Better Homes and Gardens®

SIMPLE MEXICAN COOKING

BETTER HOMES AND GARDENS ® TEST KITCHEN ®

Originally offered as *Today's Easy Mexican Cooking*

SIMPLE MEXICAN COOKING

Our seal assures you that every recipe in *Simple Mexican Cooking* has been tested in the *Better Homes and Gardens*® Test Kitchen. This means that each recipe is practical and reliable, and meets our high standards of taste appeal.

Pictured on the cover: 20-Minute Chicken Tacos (see recipe, page 56)

Project Editor: Lois White
Project Designer: Linda Bender
Recipe Development: Marlene Brown, Elena Cota
Food Stylist: Susan Brown Draudt
Prop Stylist: Robin Tucker
Photographers: DeGennaro Associates
Production Manager: Ivan McDonald

Vice President, Publishing Director: John Loughlin
Publisher: Mike Peterson
Editor-in-Chief: Don Johnson
Design Director: Jann Williams
Test Kitchen Director: Sharon Stilwell

All of us at Meredith Corporation are dedicated to providing you with the information and ideas you need to create tasty foods. We welcome your comments and suggestions. Write to us at: Simple Mexican Cooking, Meredith Custom Publishing, 1912 Grand Ave., Des Moines, IA 50309-3379.

Better Homes and Gardens®

SIMPLE MEXICAN COOKING

BETTER HOMES AND GARDENS TEST KITCHEN ®

CONTENTS

A Fiesta of Mexican Flavors 4

Appetizers Olé...12

South-of-the-Border Main Dishes...............................30

Sensational Side Dishes..64

Irresistible Sweets...82

Recipe Index 96

MEXICAN
A FIESTA OF
FLAVORS

Mexico's geographical variety, combined with a cultural legacy influenced by the Spanish, French, and the rest of Latin America, has shaped a culinary heritage that's as unique and colorful as the country itself.

More than 7,000 years of agricultural tradition, as well as a rich cultural and geographical diversity, have made Mexico a food mecca. The country's vast coastline provides an array of seafood and fish, while ranches and farms on the interior offer livestock and a cornucopia of tropical fruits and vegetables.

Explored on these pages are the staples that give Mexican cuisine its distinctive flavor as well as the unique ingredients that lend it a subtle sophistication. Experience the authentic and diverse flavors of Mexico through these tasty recipes.

Favorite Ingredients of Mexican Cooks

In every pantry in Mexico, there are ingredients that lend distinctive flavor and character to favorite native dishes. Look for these ingredients in the produce section of your supermarket or in Mexican and Oriental food stores.

Avocados—pear-shaped fruit with green skin, a large pit, and yellow-green meat. Peel and slice or dice avocados for salads. Or, mash them for guacamole, a dip and condiment. They have a mild, nutty flavor.

Cactus leaves or nopales (no-PAH-lays)—the leaves, or pads, of the prickly pear cactus. Remove the prickles with a knife, and slice or dice to use lightly steamed or sautéed. Nopales have a mild flavor, somewhat like green beans. Cactus leaves are sometimes available pickled.

Chayotes (chaw-YOTE-ees) or mirlitons—pear-shaped squash with thin, pale green skin and a slender, white seed. Their moist flesh has a mild cucumber-apple flavor. You can steam, sauté, or even bake chayotes (stuffed with meats or cheeses) just as you would zucchini.

Chorizo (chor-EE-so)—a hot, peppery Spanish sausage. Sold in bulk or stuffed into casings to make links, chorizo is made from pork or beef.

Cilantro
(sih-LON-troh), also known as coriander or Chinese parsley—a
lacy parsley with medium-green leaves. It adds a distinctive flavor to salsas, main dishes,
and sauces. Cilantro also is commonly used as a garnish.

Jicama (HE-kuh-muh) or Mexican potato—a bulbous root
vegetable with pale brown skin and white meat. Always
peel before eating and enjoy it raw, sautéed, or
shredded in salads. Jicama has a mild, sweet flavor
and crisp texture.

Mangoes—tropical oval or kidney-shaped
fruit with red-tinged green to yellow skin. The fruit's deep
golden yellow meat has a spicy peach flavor but is
more perfumy than a peach and very juicy. Mangoes
have a large, flat, oval, white inedible seed.

Masa (MAH-sah)—corn, corn flour, or the corn dough used to make tortillas and tamales. Instant masa, most commonly available in 5-pound bags, is dried corn flour that can be mixed with water to make the masa or dough.

Plantains (PLAN-tins)—a cooking fruit resembling bananas, with green to yellow to black skin that tightly adheres to the fruit. Used in savory or sweet dishes, plantains always are steamed, baked, or fried before eating. Their flavor is very mild, and they often are served in place of potatoes or rice.

Tamarindo (tah-mar-EEN-doh)—slender, dried pods from the tamarind tree, with a pulpy interior that tastes like apricots and lemons. The fruit is seeded and used in drinks, sauces, and condiments.

Tomatillos (toh-mah-TEE-yohs) or Mexican green tomatoes—small, pale green fruit covered in papery, brown husks. Their distinctive tart, lemony flavor makes them excellent for salads and salsas or salsa verde (green sauce). Tomatillos also are pickled or used in cooked dishes.

Tortillas—Mexican flat bread, made with corn or wheat flour, that is flattened into pancake shapes and baked on a griddle or skillet. Tortillas are used in tacos, tostadas, enchiladas, burritos, and other traditional dishes.

A Guide to Saying
Cheese—Mexican Style!

**Look for these cheeses in the gourmet cheese section of larger
supermarkets or in Mexican or Latin American food stores.**

Asadero—sold in flat, round slices or rolled into balls. The balls pull apart in long strands like string cheese. Its distinctive buttery flavor makes it excellent for snacks, such as quesadillas.

Chihuahua—a rich, semi-firm cheese with a mildly tangy flavor (similar to cheddar cheese) and good melting qualities. Use chihuahua in cooking and for snacks.

Cotija (coh-TEE-ya)—a firm, white, salty fresh cheese that can be substituted for Parmesan or feta cheese. It crumbles easily and can be sprinkled over salads, soups, or baked dishes.

Enchilado—a firm, dry cheese with a slightly pungent taste and a red-pepper coating. Slice, shred, or melt this cheese.

Queso Fresco (KAY-soh FRES-coh)—a mild-flavored, soft white cheese that is made from cow's milk and can be sliced or shredded. Try adding queso fresco to cooked dishes or crumble it over finished dishes for a garnish.

Panela—fresh, smooth, mozzarella-like cheese. It stays soft and creamy when melted over enchiladas or other hot dishes.

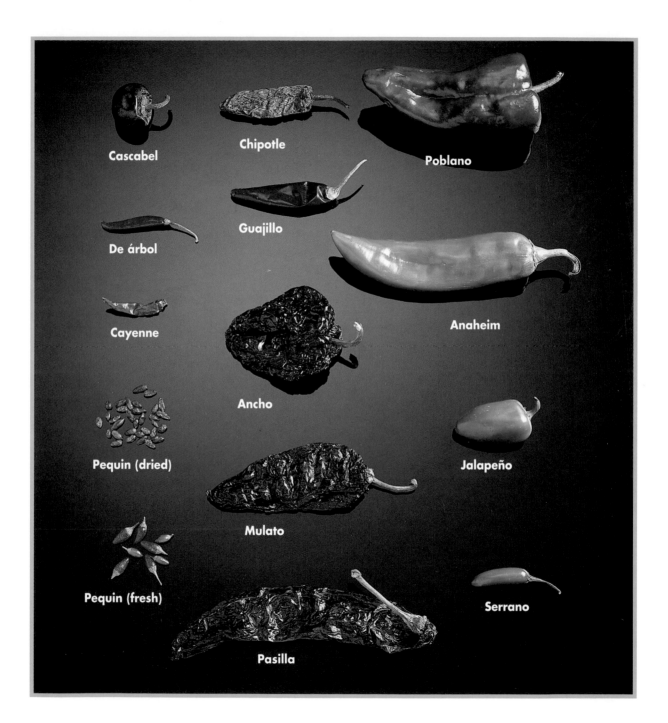

Cascabel

Chipotle

Poblano

Guajillo

De árbol

Anaheim

Cayenne

Ancho

Pequin (dried)

Jalapeño

Mulato

Pequin (fresh)

Serrano

Pasilla

Chile Pepper Choices

It's said there's a chile for every city and town in Mexico! Here are some of the most commonly used peppers. When purchasing fresh chiles, select those with firm, unblemished skins.

Anaheim or California green chile peppers—the most common of the fresh chiles. This light green pepper has a mild flavor with just a slight bite. Anaheims are 4 to 6 inches long.

Ancho—large triangular-shaped peppers with wrinkled reddish-brown skin. Anchos (which are dried poblanos) are commonly used in red chile sauces. They range from mild to medium-hot.

Cascabel—dried, round, cherry-shaped peppers with tough, dark red skin. Their flavor ranges from medium-hot to hot.

Cayenne—dried, slender, red pepper with a fiery-hot taste. It's used almost exclusively in the ground form called ground red pepper.

Chipotle—actually dried, smoked jalapeño peppers. Chipotles have a dull brown, wrinkled skin and a rich, smoky, hot flavor.

De árbol—another dried, small, slender pepper. It features a bright red skin and very hot flavor.

Guajillo—a dried, medium-long pepper with a slender shape and smooth, brick-red skin. This pepper is very hot.

Jalapeño—hot, fresh peppers with green or red skins that are 2½ to 3 inches long and about ¾ to 1 inch wide. Often pickled.

Mulato—mild to hot, triangular pepper with a wrinkled, brown-black skin. Look for dried or powdered.

Pasilla—dried, long, slender, medium-sized chiles with black-brown skins. Often combined with ancho peppers, they are very hot.

Pequin—also called "tepin chile peppers." The tiny fresh or dried chiles have an orange-red skin and are extremely hot.

Poblano—dark green chiles when fresh (deep brick-red when dried) with a mild to medium-hot flavor. They're large (3½ to 5 inches long), plump, and bell-shaped with a pointed end.

Serrano—small, slender, green or red fresh chile with a pointed end. These very hot chiles are available canned or pickled.

See pages 41 and 43 for tips on handling and peeling hot peppers.

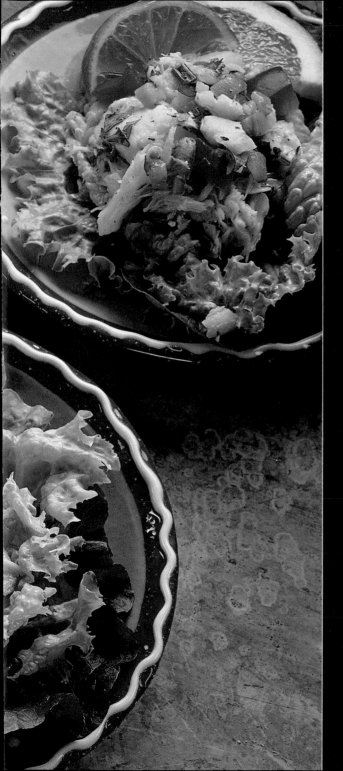

OLÉ

Whether you call them *entremeses, botanas,* or *aperitivos,* these truly Mexican-style appetizers and snacks taste wonderful, without losing anything in the translation! In Mexico, many of these foods may be served between meals, as "little meals," or as street food in the afternoon or evening, served from roving food carts and portable grills in the marketplaces of Mexico.

You can prepare some of these tasty tidbits, such as Jicama with Chili and Lime, in as little as 15 minutes. Wow your guests with such authentic appetite-teasers as Pepper-and-Cheese Quesadillas, Seviche-Style Crab and Scallops (pictured), or Garlic Soup. You'll also find your favorite embellishments, such as Homemade Salsa and Chunky Guacamole, to accent recipes throughout this book.

Melon Punch

Try serving this refreshing punch with a spicy appetizer. Along with the mint sprigs, garnish each drink with a small melon ball or two, if you like. Cut the melon balls quickly with a scalloped melon ball cutter.

Preparation Time: 20 minutes

- 4 cups cubed melon (cantaloupe, honeydew, seeded watermelon, or casaba)
- 1 cup orange juice
- ⅓ cup water
- 2 tablespoons sugar
  Ice cubes
  Fresh mint sprigs

━━ In a blender container or food processor bowl place *half* of the melon cubes and the orange juice; cover and blend or process until smooth. Strain into a pitcher.

━━ In a blender container or food processor bowl place remaining melon cubes with the water and sugar. Cover and blend or process until smooth. Strain into first mixture. Stir until combined; add ice cubes. Garnish with fresh mint sprigs. Makes about 6 (4-ounce) servings.

Per serving: 72 cal., 1 g pro., 17 g carbo., 0 g fat, 0 mg cholesterol, 1 g dietary fiber, 10 mg sodium.

Jicama with Chili and Lime

Jicama sticks dunked in chili powder are a traditional Mexican snack. Serve these with the above punch or a Mexican beer.

Preparation Time: 15 minutes

- 2 tablespoons lime juice
- ½ teaspoon chili powder
- 3 cups peeled jicama sticks
- 1 cucumber, sliced
  Lettuce leaves
  Fresh cilantro or parsley sprigs

In a small bowl combine lime juice and chili powder. Arrange jicama sticks and cucumber slices on a lettuce-lined platter. Lightly brush lime juice mixture over jicama and cucumber. Garnish with cilantro or parsley sprigs. Makes 8 servings.

*Per serving: 28 cal., 1 g pro., 6 g carbo., 0 g fat, 0 mg cholesterol,
2 g dietary fiber, 7 mg sodium.*

Nachos with Chorizo

We've baked the chips in this recipe to substitute for the fried chips traditionally used. If you're in a time crunch, you can omit the chip preparation and use purchased tortilla chips.

Preparation Time: 25 minutes
Baking Time: 4 minutes

6 **6-inch corn or flour tortillas**
  Cooking oil
12 **ounces bulk chorizo or Italian sausage**
2 **cups shredded Monterey Jack cheese or cheddar cheese (8 ounces)**
½ **cup sliced green onions**
  Homemade Salsa or Tomatillo Salsa (see recipes, pages 16-17)

Stack tortillas; cut the stack into six wedges. On two 12-inch pizza pans or baking sheets arrange wedges in a single layer. Brush lightly with oil (about 1 tablespoon). Bake in a 350° oven for 12 to 15 minutes or until golden and crisp.

Meanwhile, in a skillet cook sausage until brown. Drain off fat. Remove from heat. Sprinkle the meat over tortilla wedges. Sprinkle with cheese and green onions. Bake in a 350° oven about 4 minutes or until cheese melts. Serve immediately with desired salsa. Makes 12 servings.

*Per serving (without salsa): 212 cal., 11 g pro., 8 g carbo., 15 g fat,
36 mg cholesterol, 1 g dietary fiber, 388 mg sodium.*

Homemade Salsa

Preparation Time: 15 minutes
Chilling Time: 1 to 48 hours

1   **large tomato, chopped (1 cup)**
1   **small onion, chopped (⅓ cup)**
3   **green onions, finely chopped (⅓ cup)**
2   **tablespoons finely chopped, pickled jalapeño pepper**
2   **tablespoons vinegar**

— Combine all ingredients. Cover; chill for 1 hour. Makes 1¾ cups.

Per tablespoon: 2 cal., 0 g pro., 1 g carbo., 0 g fat, 0 mg cholesterol,
0 g dietary fiber, 9 mg sodium.

Red Chile Sauce

Preparation Time: 10 minutes
Standing Time: 45 minutes
Cooking Time: 10 minutes

6   **dried ancho peppers or ¼ cup chili powder**
2   **tablespoons cooking oil**
1   **14½-ounce can tomatoes**
2   **cloves garlic**
2   **teaspoons sugar**
½   **teaspoon salt**
½   **teaspoon dried oregano, crushed**
¼   **teaspoon ground cumin**

— If using dried peppers, omit cooking oil; rinse peppers in water. Slit peppers lengthwise; discard stems and seeds. With a knife or scissors, cut peppers into small pieces. In a bowl add pepper pieces to boiling water; let stand for 45 to 60 minutes to soften. Drain well. (If using chili powder, in a saucepan cook and stir chili powder in hot oil over medium-low heat for 4 minutes.) Place *undrained* tomatoes in a blender container or food processor bowl. Add drained peppers or chili powder mixture and garlic. Cover and blend or process until smooth. Transfer mixture to a saucepan. Stir in sugar, salt, oregano, and cumin. Bring to boiling; reduce heat. If using dried peppers, cover and

Homemade Salsa

simmer for 10 minutes. (For chili powder, simmer, uncovered, about 10 minutes or until mixture is slightly thickened.) Store, tightly covered, in the refrigerator for up to 2 weeks. Serve warm as a topper for main dishes. Makes 1⅔ to 2⅓ cups.

Per tablespoon: 14 cal., 0 g pro., 1 g carbo., 1 g fat, 0 mg cholesterol, 1 g dietary fiber, 64 mg sodium.

Tomatillo Salsa

Serrano peppers have more fire than jalapeños, so adjust the amount you use according to your taste.

Preparation Time: 15 minutes
Chilling Time: 1 to 48 hours

- **8** ounces large fresh tomatillos, husked and finely chopped (1 cup)
- **1** stalk celery, finely chopped (½ cup)
- **1** small onion, finely chopped (⅓ cup)
- **2** fresh serrano or jalapeño peppers, finely chopped
- **2** tablespoons snipped fresh cilantro or parsley
- **2** cloves garlic, minced

Combine all ingredients and ¼ teaspoon *salt*. Cover and chill in the refrigerator up to 2 days. Makes about 1½ cups.

Per tablespoon: 4 cal., 0 g pro., 1 g carbo., 0 g fat, 0 mg cholesterol, 0 g dietary fiber, 35 mg sodium.

Red Chile Sauce *Tomatillo Salsa*

Sausage-Stuffed Mushrooms

Preparation Time: 30 minutes
Baking Time: 20 minutes

- **24** large mushrooms
- **8** ounces bulk chorizo or Italian sausage
- **1** cup shredded Monterey Jack cheese (4 ounces)
- **¼** cup salsa or taco sauce
- **¼** cup thinly sliced green onions

▬ Wash mushrooms; drain. Remove stems from mushrooms; set caps aside. (Reserve stems for use in another recipe.)

▬ In a small skillet cook sausage until brown, stirring to break up any large pieces. Drain off fat. Stir together the cooked sausage and the cheese. Fill each mushroom cap with about *1 teaspoon* of the sausage mixture. Place mushrooms in a 15x10x1-inch baking pan. Spoon salsa or taco sauce over top.

▬ Bake in a 350° oven for 20 to 25 minutes or until heated through. Sprinkle with green onions. Makes 24 appetizers.

Per appetizer: 57 cal., 3 g pro., 1 g carbo., 4 g fat, 11 mg cholesterol,
0 g dietary fiber, 130 mg sodium.

Chunky Guacamole

You can make this ahead by increasing the lemon juice to 1 tablespoon. Cover and chill the "guac" until serving time.
Preparation Time: 15 minutes

- **2** large ripe avocados, halved, seeded, peeled, and chopped
- **2** green onions, sliced
- **1** small onion, chopped
- **1** teaspoon lemon juice
- **1** teaspoon olive oil or salad oil

Dash salt
Dash pepper
1 **medium tomato, chopped**
Fresh cilantro sprigs or additional chopped tomato (optional)

▬ In a medium mixing bowl combine the avocados, onions, lemon juice, oil, salt, and pepper. Stir in the chopped tomato. Transfer to a serving bowl. Garnish with cilantro or additional chopped tomato, if desired. Makes 2 cups (16 servings).

Per serving: 54 cal., 1 g pro., 3 g carbo., 5 g fat, 0 mg cholesterol,
1 g dietary fiber, 12 mg sodium.

Toasted Chili Nuts

Preparation Time: 15 minutes
Baking Time: 12 minutes

2 **tablespoons margarine or butter**
2 **tablespoons Worcestershire sauce**
1 **teaspoon chili powder**
¼ **teaspoon onion salt**
¼ **teaspoon ground red pepper**
2 **cups walnut or pecan halves or pieces**

▬ In a saucepan combine margarine or butter, Worcestershire sauce, chili powder, onion salt, and ground red pepper. Heat and stir until margarine melts. In 9x9x2-inch baking pan spread walnuts or pecans. Drizzle margarine mixture over nuts and toss to lightly coat.

▬ Bake in a 350° oven for 12 to 15 minutes or until toasted, stirring occasionally. Spread mixture on foil; cool. Store in an airtight container. Makes 2 cups (16 servings).

Per serving: 96 cal., 2 g pro., 3 g carbo., 9 g fat, 0 mg cholesterol,
1 g dietary fiber, 61 mg sodium.

Pepper-and-Cheese Quesadillas

If you want 14 to 16 smaller servings of these quesadillas, you can make them with seven or
eight 6-inch flour tortillas instead of the 8-inch tortillas.
Preparation Time: 20 minutes
Cooking Time: 3 to 4 minutes for two

1   fresh medium poblano or Anaheim pepper or 2 jalapeño peppers
2½ cups shredded Monterey Jack cheese (10 ounces)
5   8-inch flour tortillas
1   small tomato, chopped
1   small onion, chopped
     Chunky Guacamole (see recipe, page 18) (optional)
     Homemade Salsa (see recipe, page 16) (optional)
     Assorted chile peppers (optional)
     Fresh cilantro sprigs (optional)

Cut pepper in half, remove seeds, and remove membrane if milder flavor is desired. Cut pepper into thin slivers. Sprinkle ½ *cup* of the cheese over *half of each* tortilla. Sprinkle pepper slivers, tomato, and onion equally over cheese. Fold tortillas in half, pressing gently.

In a large skillet or on a griddle cook quesadillas, two at a time, over medium heat about 3 to 4 minutes or until lightly browned, turning once. Remove quesadillas from the skillet and place on a baking sheet. Keep warm in a 300° oven. Repeat with remaining quesadillas.

To serve, cut quesadillas in half. Serve with Chunky Guacamole or Homemade Salsa, if desired. Garnish with chile peppers and cilantro, if desired. Makes 10 servings.

Per serving (without sauce): 171 cal., 9 g pro., 12 g carbo., 10 g fat,
25 mg cholesterol, 1 g dietary fiber, 238 mg sodium.

Garlic Soup

The garlic flavor is mellow and pleasant in this simple soup, which could be served as a light lunch with a tossed green salad.

Preparation Time: 30 minutes
Cooking Time: 5 minutes

2	tablespoons olive oil
6	large cloves garlic, minced
4	to 5 slices French bread, cubed (2 cups)
4	cups chicken or beef broth
½	teaspoon chili powder
4	eggs
	Mexican grating cheese, grated (optional)
	Pepper (optional)

■■■ In a large skillet heat olive oil over medium heat. Add garlic and brown slightly, about 1 minute. Remove garlic, reserving oil in skillet; set garlic aside. Add cubed bread to oil in skillet and toast to make croutons, stirring frequently. Remove croutons from skillet.

■■■ In a medium saucepan combine broth, reserved garlic, and chili powder. Bring to boiling; reduce heat. Cover and simmer about 5 minutes to blend flavors.

■■■ Carefully break *1 egg* into a small dish. Gently slide the egg into the simmering broth, holding the lip of the dish as close to the broth as possible. Repeat with remaining eggs, allowing each egg an equal amount of space. Simmer eggs, uncovered, about 5 minutes or until yolk is just set.

■■■ Use a slotted spoon to remove the poached eggs and place each in a soup bowl. Add heated broth and serve immediately. Pass the croutons. If desired, garnish with grated Mexican cheese and season to taste with pepper. Makes 4 appetizer servings.

Per serving: 270 cal., 12 g pro., 23 g carbo., 15 g fat, 213 mg cholesterol, 1 g dietary fiber, 1,240 mg sodium.

Vermicelli Soup

Preparation Time: 10 minutes
Cooking Time: 15 minutes

1   6-ounce can tomato paste
⅓   cup water
⅓   cup chopped onion
2   tablespoons snipped fresh cilantro or parsley
2   cloves garlic, minced
1   tablespoon cooking oil
2   ounces vermicelli, broken into 2-inch pieces
2   14½-ounce cans chicken broth
¼   teaspoon pepper
    Grated Parmesan or Romano cheese

▬ In a blender container or food processor bowl combine tomato paste, water, onion, cilantro or parsley, and garlic. Cover and blend or process until mixture is nearly smooth. Set aside.

▬ In a large saucepan heat oil. Cook and stir vermicelli in hot oil over low heat about 4 minutes or until golden brown. Carefully add tomato mixture and chicken broth. Bring to boiling; reduce heat. Cover and simmer about 15 minutes or until vermicelli is tender but still firm. Stir in pepper. Sprinkle each serving with Parmesan or Romano cheese. Makes 6 appetizer servings.

Per serving: 114 cal., 5 g pro., 15 g carbo., 5 g fat, 2 mg cholesterol,
1 g dietary fiber, 657 mg sodium.

Homemade Chili Powder

Combine 1 ounce ground chiles* (about ⅓ cup); ¾ to 1 teaspoon dried oregano, finely crushed; ¾ teaspoon garlic powder; ½ to ¾ teaspoon ground cumin; and ½ teaspoon ground pepper. Cover tightly to store. Use in recipes calling for chili powder. Makes about ⅓ cup.

*Use one or a combination of several ground chiles when preparing chili powder. Varieties of milder chiles include California and New Mexico.

Chilled Avocado Soup

This classic cold soup is a great make-ahead and a refreshing change from gazpacho, another popular chilled soup.

Preparation Time: 20 minutes
Chilling Time: 2 hours

3	ripe avocados, halved, seeded, peeled, and cut up
3	cups chicken, beef, or vegetable broth
3	tablespoons dry sherry or dry white wine
2	tablespoons lemon juice
1	green onion, finely chopped
	Dash salt
	Dash white pepper
	Dash ground red pepper
1	8-ounce carton dairy sour cream or light dairy sour cream
⅓	cup finely snipped chives
	Avocado, halved, seeded, peeled, and cut into small cubes

▬ In a blender container or food processor bowl place *half* of the 3 cut-up avocados, *half* of the broth, the sherry, lemon juice, onion, salt, white pepper, and ground red pepper. Cover and blend or process at low speed until smooth and satiny. Pour into a bowl. Repeat with remaining avocado and broth; add to mixture in bowl. Stir in the sour cream until well mixed.

▬ Chill for 2 to 24 hours. To serve, ladle into chilled soup cups. Garnish with chives and avocado cubes. Makes 8 appetizer servings.

Per serving: 240 cal., 4 g pro., 10 g carbo., 22 g fat, 13 mg cholesterol, 3 g dietary fiber, 402 mg sodium.

Pumpkin and Tomato Soup

Preparation Time: 25 minutes
Standing Time: 45 minutes
Cooking Time: 20 minutes

1	dried ancho or pasilla pepper
1	cup boiling water

1½ cups chicken broth
¾ cup canned pumpkin
¼ cup chopped onion
1 clove garlic, minced
1 small tomato, chopped
½ cup half-and-half or light cream

▬ Rinse dried pepper in water. Slit pepper lengthwise; discard stem and seeds. With a knife or scissors, cut pepper into small pieces. In a bowl add pepper pieces to boiling water; cover and let stand for 45 to 60 minutes to soften. Strain liquid; reserve ½ *cup* of the liquid and the pepper pieces.

▬ In a medium saucepan combine reserved pepper liquid and pepper, chicken broth, pumpkin, onion, and garlic. Bring to boiling; reduce heat. Cover and simmer for 15 minutes or until onion is tender. Cool slightly.

▬ In a blender container or food processor bowl transfer *half* of the pumpkin mixture. Cover; blend or process until smooth. Repeat with remaining mixture. Return all to saucepan. Stir in tomato and cream. Cook for 3 to 5 minutes or until hot, but *do not boil*. Makes 4 appetizer servings.

Per serving: 73 cal., 2 g pro., 7 g carbo., 4 g fat, 11 mg cholesterol,
1 g dietary fiber, 408 mg sodium.

Pumpkin and Tomato Soup

Seviche-Style Crab and Scallops

You can substitute a 12-ounce cooked crab leg for frozen crabmeat. Just remove the meat from the shell and chop. (Pictured on pages 12–13.)

Preparation Time: 20 minutes
Marinating Time: 30 minutes
Chilling Time: 2 hours

4 ounces fresh or frozen scallops
1 6-ounce package frozen crabmeat, thawed and cut into bite-size pieces
¼ cup lime juice
¼ cup orange juice
¼ cup sliced green onions
1 4-ounce can diced green chile peppers, drained
2 tablespoons olive oil or salad oil
2 tablespoons snipped fresh cilantro or parsley
½ teaspoon dried oregano, crushed
¼ teaspoon salt
¼ teaspoon pepper
1 medium tomato, chopped
Lettuce leaves
Lime wedges and/or orange slices (optional)

▬ Thaw scallops, if frozen. Cut any large scallops in half. In a medium saucepan cook scallops in boiling water about 1 minute or until opaque. Drain and rinse under cool water to stop cooking. Place scallops and crab in a small nonmetallic bowl.

▬ For marinade, in a small bowl stir together lime juice and orange juice. Pour marinade over seafood in bowl. Gently toss together to evenly distribute marinade. Cover and chill for 30 minutes (do not chill longer or seafood will toughen). Drain scallops and crab, discarding marinade. In a medium mixing bowl stir together green onions, chile peppers, olive oil or salad oil, cilantro or parsley, oregano, salt, and pepper. Gently stir in scallops and crabmeat until combined. Cover and chill at least 2 hours.

▬ Just before serving, toss chopped tomato with seafood mixture. Arrange lettuce leaves on a serving platter. Spoon seafood mixture over lettuce. Garnish with lime wedges and/or orange slices, if desired. Makes 6 servings.

Per serving: 107 cal., 9 g pro., 6 g carbo., 6 g fat, 33 mg cholesterol,
1 g dietary fiber, 200 mg sodium.

OLÉ

Seafood-Stuffed Chiles

*This dish is traditionally served along the coast of Baja. You can substitute an
8-ounce cooked crab leg for the frozen crabmeat.*

Preparation Time: 30 minutes
Cooking Time: 15 minutes

1   7-ounce can or two 4-ounce cans whole green chile peppers, rinsed
        and drained (6 peppers)
1   tablespoon cooking oil
¼   cup chopped onion
1   clove garlic, minced
8   ounces medium-size shrimp in shells, peeled, deveined, and chopped
        (5 ounces shelled)
4   ounces frozen crabmeat, thawed and flaked
½   teaspoon dried oregano, crushed
¼   teaspoon ground cumin
1¼   cups shredded Monterey Jack cheese (5 ounces)

▬   Cut each pepper open by slitting down one side. Remove seeds and discard.
Pat peppers dry with paper towels; set aside.

▬   In a medium skillet heat cooking oil. Cook onion and garlic in hot oil for
2 minutes. Add shrimp; cook and stir about 3 minutes or until shrimp turn opaque. Stir in
crabmeat, oregano, and cumin; remove from heat. Stir in *½ cup* of the cheese. Spoon
stuffing mixture onto *half* of each pepper; fold other half of pepper over filling.

▬   In a 2-quart square baking dish arrange the stuffed peppers. Sprinkle
remaining cheese over peppers. Cover and bake in a 375° oven for 15 to 20 minutes or
until cheese is melted and filling is heated through. Makes 6 servings.

*Per serving: 167 cal., 16 g pro., 3 g carbo., 10 g fat, 95 mg cholesterol,
1 g dietary fiber, 630 mg sodium.*

Josefinas

Preparation Time: 25 minutes

1   small baguette (about 12 inches long)
½   cup shredded Monterey Jack cheese (2 ounces)
¼   cup dairy sour cream
1   4-ounce can diced green chile peppers, drained
½   small onion, finely chopped
2   cloves garlic, minced
    Paprika

▬ Split baguette lengthwise. Toast under broiler about 4 inches from heat for 1 to 2 minutes. In a mixing bowl stir together cheese, sour cream, peppers, onion, and garlic. Spread mixture evenly to edges of toasted baguette halves. Sprinkle lightly with paprika.

▬ Place under broiler about 4 inches from heat and broil for 2 to 3 minutes or until golden and puffy. Remove from broiler and cut each into 8 pieces. Serve immediately as a hot appetizer. Makes 16 appetizers.

Per appetizer: 73 cal., 3 g pro., 10 g carbo., 2 g fat, 5 mg cholesterol,
1 g dietary fiber, 128 mg sodium.

Fried Cheese

You'll get better results from frying if you strain out the crumbs in the oil between batches of cheese. Use a long-handled strainer or a large slotted spoon.
Preparation Time: 45 minutes

1   pound Monterey Jack cheese or Monterey Jack cheese
      with jalapeño peppers
1   cup milk
1   cup all-purpose flour
1   cup fine dry seasoned bread crumbs
    Cooking oil for frying
    Salsa

▬ Cut cheese into 1-inch cubes or rectangular sticks about 1½x¾ inches. Place cheese pieces in a bowl; pour the milk over the cheese, coating cheese thoroughly. Remove cheese from milk and coat with flour. Quickly coat in milk again and roll in bread crumbs.

■ Meanwhile, in a heavy medium or large saucepan heat 2 to 3 inches of oil to 365°. Quickly fry a few pieces of cheese at a time in oil about 1 minute or until golden brown. Remove cheese with a slotted spoon. Drain well on paper towels. Serve with salsa that has been heated. Makes about 20 appetizers.

Per appetizer: 160 cal., 7 g pro., 9 g carbo., 11 g fat, 20 mg cholesterol,
0 g dietary fiber, 305 mg sodium.

Chile con Queso
Preparation Time: 40 minutes

1   **cup finely chopped onion**
2   **tablespoons margarine or butter**
4   **medium tomatoes, peeled, seeded, and chopped**
2   **4-ounce cans diced green chile peppers, drained**
2   **cups shredded cheddar cheese (8 ounces)**
2   **cups shredded Monterey Jack cheese (8 ounces)**
    Milk
    Assorted fresh vegetable dippers

■ In a large saucepan cook onion in margarine or butter until tender but not brown. Stir in tomatoes and chile peppers. Simmer, uncovered, for 10 minutes.

■ Add shredded cheddar and Monterey Jack cheeses a little at a time, stirring just until melted. Stir in a little milk if mixture becomes too thick. Heat through. Transfer dip to a serving bowl. Serve with desired dippers. Makes about 3½ cups or 14 (¼-cup) servings.

Per serving (without dippers): 155 cal., 9 g pro., 4 g carbo., 12 g fat,
31 mg cholesterol, 1 g dietary fiber, 394 mg sodium.

MAIN
SOUTH-OF-THE-BORD
DISHES

In the full Mexican meal, or *comida,* the main course consists of a meat, poultry, or fish dish. The meats, poultry, and fish or seafood are stewed, roasted, grilled, or slow-cooked with an amazing variety of ingredients. Many of these dishes are so delicious and easy to prepare that you'll not only want to try them, you'll make them part of your culinary repertoire, too!

Sample our chicken dishes with olives and raisins, mushrooms, or oranges. Try fish in tacos or a traditional Snapper Veracruz. Savor pork stewed with vegetables or shredded in the Mexican style. Don't miss the Stuffed Flank Steak Roll (pictured) or the meatless dishes featuring cheese, beans, or eggs.

Stuffed Flank Steak Roll

Try this meat topped with sour cream sauce for a special occasion. (Pictured on pages 30–31.)

Preparation Time: 35 minutes

Roasting Time: 1 hour

1	1½-pound beef flank steak
1	beaten egg
1	10-ounce package frozen chopped spinach, thawed and well drained
½	cup chopped red sweet pepper
¼	cup finely chopped onion
2	tablespoons canned chopped green chile peppers, drained
2	tablespoons pine nuts or slivered almonds
1	clove garlic, minced
¼	teaspoon salt
¼	teaspoon pepper
½	cup beef broth
2	tablespoons all-purpose flour
1	8-ounce carton dairy sour cream

▬ Score one side of the meat by making shallow cuts at 1-inch intervals diagonally across steak in a diamond pattern. Turn over and repeat on other side. With a meat mallet, pound steak into a 12x8-inch rectangle, working from center to edges.

▬ In a mixing bowl combine egg, spinach, sweet pepper, onion, chile peppers, nuts, garlic, salt, and pepper. Mix thoroughly. Spread evenly over meat. Roll up steak from a short side and tie with kitchen string.

▬ In a 13x9x2-inch baking pan place meat roll on a rack. Pour beef broth over meat. Cover pan with foil and roast in a 350° oven for 50 minutes or until meat is tender. Uncover and roast for 8 to 10 minutes longer to brown the top of the meat.

▬ Remove roast from pan. Cover meat and keep warm. In a small saucepan stir flour into sour cream. Skim fat from the pan drippings. Measure ½ cup drippings; add water, if necessary, to make ½ cup liquid. Stir drippings into the sour cream mixture. Cook and stir over medium heat until mixture is thickened and bubbly. Cook and stir 1 minute more. Slice meat and serve with sour cream sauce. Makes 6 servings.

Per serving: 312 cal., 28 g pro., 8 g carbo., 19 g fat, 110 mg cholesterol,
2 g dietary fiber, 301 mg sodium.

Peppered Flank Steak

Preparation Time: 15 minutes
Marinating Time: 4 hours
Broiling Time: 14 minutes

1   **cup orange juice**
1   **teaspoon coarsely ground black pepper**
2   **cloves garlic, minced**
¼   **teaspoon ground cumin**
1   **1½-pound beef flank steak**

━━ In a bowl combine orange juice, pepper, garlic, and cumin. Place meat in a shallow nonmetallic bowl. Pour orange juice mixture over meat. Turn meat to evenly distribute marinade. Cover and chill for 4 hours or overnight, turning meat occasionally.

━━ Remove meat from marinade, reserving marinade. Place meat on the unheated rack of a broiler pan. Broil 3 inches from the heat for 7 minutes. Turn meat over, brushing both sides with marinade. Discard remaining marinade. Broil meat 7 to 9 minutes longer. Season to taste with salt, if desired. Slice meat thinly across the grain. Makes 6 servings.

Per serving: 182 cal., 23 g pro., 2 g carbo., 9 g fat, 57 mg cholesterol,
0 g dietary fiber, 71 mg sodium.

Warming Tortillas

Heating tortillas softens them to make them easier to fold or roll. You can heat tortillas several different ways.

- To oven-warm tortillas, wrap a stack of tortillas in foil and place the package on the oven rack in a 350° oven for 10 minutes.
- To microwave-warm tortillas, place four 6- to 7-inch flour tortillas between microwave-safe paper towels. Micro-cook on 100% power (high) for 45 to 60 seconds or until softened.
- To serve hot tortillas, try a tortilla warmer—a round container with a tight-fitting cover that holds a flat stack of heated tortillas. You can place it on your table and allow diners to help themselves.

Mexican-Style Shredded Pork

Pork prepared this way is called carnitas. It's used for tacos and tostadas.

Preparation Time: 20 minutes

Cooking Time: 2½ hours

1	2-pound boneless pork shoulder
1	large onion, quartered
8	cloves garlic, minced
2	teaspoons ground coriander
2	teaspoons ground cumin
2	teaspoons dried oregano, crushed
4	bay leaves
2	to 4 fresh jalapeño peppers, finely chopped (½ cup)
1	teaspoon salt

▬ In a large saucepan combine pork and enough *water* (about 4 cups) to nearly cover pork. Add remaining ingredients. Bring to boiling; reduce heat. Cover and simmer for 2½ to 3 hours or until very tender. Remove meat from liquid. Strain liquid through a 100% cotton cheesecloth-lined colander, reserving liquid. Shred pork, discarding any fat. Return meat to saucepan; add enough reserved liquid to moisten. Cook until heated through; drain before serving. Makes about 14 ounces meat (about 3 cups).

Per ounce: 91 cal., 11 g pro., 2 g carbo., 4 g fat, 37 mg cholesterol,
1 g dietary fiber, 257 mg sodium.

Pork Tostadas: Prepare *Mexican-Style Shredded Pork* as directed above. Combine 2 cups shredded *lettuce* and 1 large *avocado*, halved, seeded, peeled, and cubed; set aside.

▬ In a heavy skillet heat about ¼ inch of *cooking oil.* Fry 8 *flour tortillas,* one at a time, in hot oil about 30 seconds on each side or until crisp and golden brown. Drain on paper towels. Keep tortillas warm in a 300° oven while frying remaining ones. Toss pork with ½ cup *taco sauce.*

▬ Heat one 16-ounce can *refried beans.* To serve, place tortillas on plates. Spread some of the beans onto each tortilla. Top with the lettuce mixture, pork mixture, 8 quartered *cherry tomatoes,* and 1 cup shredded *cheddar* or *Monterey Jack cheese* (4 ounces). Makes 8 servings.

Per serving: 375 cal., 27 g pro., 19 g carbo., 22 g fat, 80 mg cholesterol,
6 g dietary fiber, 849 mg sodium.

Pork-Stuffed Chayotes

You can peel chayotes with a vegetable peeler as you would a potato or a zucchini. The seed in the center is white, long, and slender, and can be cut out with a paring knife.

Preparation Time: 20 minutes

Baking Time: 32 minutes

4	medium chayotes or zucchini (7 to 9 ounces each)
½	cup sliced green onions
½	cup chopped green sweet pepper
1	tablespoon olive oil or cooking oil
1½	cups Mexican-Style Shredded Pork (see recipe, page 35) or shredded cooked pork (about 6 ounces)
4	ounces sliced Monterey Jack or cheddar cheese
3	cups Mexican Rice (see recipe, page 70)

▬ Peel chayotes, if desired. Halve chayotes or zucchini lengthwise; remove seeds from chayotes. Place vegetables in a steamer basket over simmering water. Cook, covered, until tender, for 15 to 20 minutes for chayotes and for 10 to 15 minutes for zucchini. Remove vegetables from steamer; turn cut side down on paper towels and drain.

▬ Scoop out interior of chayotes or zucchini, leaving a ¼- to ½-inch-thick shell; finely chop the pulp. In a small skillet cook chopped chayote or zucchini, green onions, and green pepper in hot oil for 5 minutes or until tender. Stir in shredded pork; heat through. Remove from heat.

▬ In a 2-quart rectangular baking dish place chayote or zucchini shells, cut side up. Spoon pork mixture into shells, mounding slightly. Cover; bake in a 375° oven for 30 minutes. Uncover; top with cheese. Return to oven until cheese is melted. Serve with hot Mexican Rice. Makes 4 servings.

Per serving (with rice): 503 cal., 30 g pro., 43 g carbo., 24 g fat, 90 mg cholesterol, 4 g dietary fiber, 926 mg sodium.

Meatball Soup

To save time, prepare the vegetables while the meatballs simmer in the broth.

Preparation Time: 30 minutes

Cooking Time: 12 minutes

1 slightly beaten egg
3 tablespoons long grain rice
6 fresh mint leaves, finely chopped (1 tablespoon)
¼ teaspoon salt
⅛ teaspoon pepper
1 pound lean ground beef or pork
4 cups chicken, beef, or vegetable broth
1 cup frozen cut green beans
1 medium onion, thinly sliced
2 medium tomatoes, chopped
3 carrots, sliced diagonally
¾ cup frozen peas
3 cloves garlic, minced
   Snipped fresh cilantro (optional)
   Salsa (optional)

▬▬▬ In a medium mixing bowl combine the egg, *uncooked* rice, mint, salt, and pepper. Stir in the ground meat and mix well. Shape mixture into 1-inch meatballs (about the size of a radish).

▬▬▬ In a large saucepan bring broth to boiling. Add meatballs and simmer, covered, for 15 to 20 minutes or until meat and rice are cooked.

▬▬▬ Add beans, onion, tomatoes, carrots, peas, and garlic to the soup mixture. Cook, covered, for 12 to 15 minutes or until vegetables are crisp-tender. Ladle soup into bowls and serve with snipped cilantro and salsa, if desired. Makes 6 servings.

Per serving: 260 cal., 22 g pro., 17 g carbo., 12 g fat, 96 mg cholesterol, 4 g dietary fiber, 816 mg sodium.

Chiles in Nut Sauce

Preparation Time: 40 minutes
Baking Time: 20 minutes

- 1 **pound ground pork**
- 1 **small onion, chopped**
- 1 **clove garlic, minced**
- 1 **cup sliced, peeled fresh peaches or one 8½- or 8¾-ounce can peach slices, drained**
- 1 **medium pear, peeled, halved, and cored**
- 1 **8-ounce can tomato sauce**
- ¼ **cup raisins**
- ½ **teaspoon salt**
- ¼ **teaspoon ground cinnamon**
- 6 **fresh large poblano peppers or green sweet peppers**
- ¼ **cup walnuts**
- ¼ **cup blanched almonds**
- 1 **8-ounce carton dairy sour cream**
- ¼ **cup milk**
- ⅛ **teaspoon ground cinnamon**
  Dash salt
  Dash pepper

▬ In a skillet cook pork, onion, and garlic until meat is brown and onion is tender. Drain off excess fat. Chop peaches and pear; add fruit to meat along with tomato sauce, raisins, the ½ teaspoon salt, and the ¼ teaspoon cinnamon. Simmer mixture, uncovered, for 10 minutes.

▬ Meanwhile, remove stems from peppers, if desired; cut a lengthwise slit in side of each pepper and remove seeds and veins. In a Dutch oven cook peppers in lightly salted boiling water about 10 minutes or until crisp-tender; drain. Spoon meat filling into peppers. In a 2-quart rectangular baking dish place stuffed peppers. Bake in a 350° oven for 20 minutes or until heated through.

▬ Meanwhile, for nut sauce, in a blender container or with a mortar and pestle, grind walnuts and almonds until fine. In a bowl combine sour cream and milk. Stir in nuts, the ⅛ teaspoon cinnamon, dash salt, and dash pepper. Serve with peppers. Serves 6.

Per serving: 374 cal., 20 g pro., 25 g carbo., 23 g fat, 72 mg cholesterol, 5 g dietary fiber, 491 mg sodium.

Pork Stew

If a chipotle pepper is not available, substitute 1 jalapeño pepper and add 1 to 2 drops liquid smoke. Canned chipotle pepper is available in ethnic food stores and supermarkets. Or, soften a dried chipotle pepper by adding boiling water and soaking for 45 to 60 minutes. Drain before using.

Preparation Time: 40 minutes
Cooking Time: 45 minutes

1½ pounds boneless pork shoulder roast
3   tablespoons all-purpose flour
4   ounces chorizo
2   medium tomatoes, peeled and chopped
1   medium onion, finely chopped
3   cloves garlic, minced
½   chipotle pepper, chopped
¾   teaspoon salt
½   teaspoon dried oregano, crushed
⅛   teaspoon pepper
4   cups water
12   ounces whole tiny new potatoes
3   medium carrots, cut into 1-inch pieces
2   fresh ears of corn, husked and cut into 1-inch pieces
8   ounces green beans, cut into 1-inch pieces

▬ Trim fat from pork and cut the meat into ¾-inch cubes. Coat meat with flour; set aside. Remove casing from chorizo, if necessary. In a large skillet cook chorizo several minutes, stirring the chorizo frequently. Add pork and cook until brown. Drain off fat.

▬ Add tomatoes, onion, garlic, chipotle pepper, salt, oregano, and pepper. Add water, then add potatoes, carrots, and corn. Bring to boiling; reduce heat. Cover and simmer over low heat for 20 minutes. Add beans. Simmer, covered, for 25 minutes more or until meat and vegetables are tender. Makes 6 servings.

Per serving: 410 cal., 28 g pro., 37 g carbo., 18 g fat, 85 mg cholesterol, 6 g dietary fiber, 529 mg sodium.

Chicken Dry Soup

Preparation Time: 20 minutes

Cooking Time: 20 minutes

1 cup chopped carrot

1 chayote, peeled, seeded, and chopped or 1½ cups chopped zucchini

2 cloves garlic, minced

1 tablespoon olive oil or cooking oil

1 cup long grain rice

½ cup chopped onion

2 14½-ounce cans chicken broth

1 medium tomato, chopped

½ teaspoon dried oregano, crushed

1½ cups shredded cooked chicken or pork

■■■ In a large saucepan cook carrot, chayote or zucchini, and garlic in hot olive oil or cooking oil for 5 minutes. Add *uncooked* rice and onion; cook and stir 5 minutes more.

■■■ Stir in broth, tomato, and oregano. Bring to boiling; reduce heat. Cover and simmer for 20 minutes or until rice is tender and most of the liquid is absorbed. Stir in chicken or pork; heat through. Makes 4 servings.

Per serving: 371 cal., 22 g pro., 48 g carbo., 10 g fat, 47 mg cholesterol,
3 g dietary fiber, 959 mg sodium.

Safe Handling of Fresh Chile Peppers

Chile peppers contain volatile oils that can burn your skin, lips, and eyes. So, when you're handling or seeding hot peppers, cover one or both of your hands with plastic bags or gloves. If you've used your bare hands to touch the hot peppers in the process of chopping them, be sure to wash your hands and nails thoroughly with soapy water before touching your eyes or face.

It is commonly thought that the seeds of hot peppers carry the heat. However, it's the inner membranes and ribs of the pepper that hold most of the fire. So, for milder flavor, remove the membranes, ribs, and seeds of the peppers before using.

Chicken and Lime Soup with Tortillas

To trim even more time, take advantage of deli-roasted chicken. Also, try using a vegetable peeler to remove the peel from the orange.

Preparation Time: 45 minutes

½ cup chopped onion
½ cup chopped green sweet pepper
1 clove garlic, minced
1 tablespoon olive oil or cooking oil
1 large tomato, chopped
½ teaspoon dried oregano, crushed
6 cups chicken broth
4 1½x1-inch strips orange peel
3 tablespoons lime juice
2 cups shredded cooked chicken or turkey
2 6-inch corn or flour tortillas
Cooking oil
Thin lime slices
Pickled serrano peppers, rinsed, seeded, and chopped
Cracked black pepper (optional)

▬▬ In a large saucepan cook onion, green pepper, and garlic in hot oil until tender but not brown. Stir in tomato and oregano. Stir in chicken broth; bring to boiling. Stir orange peel and lime juice into broth. Reduce heat. Cover and simmer for 20 minutes. Remove orange peel. Stir in shredded chicken or turkey; heat through.

▬▬ Meanwhile, cut tortillas in half, then cut crosswise into ½-inch-wide strips. In a heavy skillet heat ½ inch oil over medium-high heat. Fry tortilla strips in hot oil for 40 to 45 seconds or until crisp and light brown. Drain on paper towels. Divide fried tortilla strips among soup bowls. Ladle soup over strips and garnish with thin slices of lime. Serve with pickled peppers and cracked pepper, if desired. Makes 4 to 6 servings.

Per serving: 439 cal., 26 g pro., 19 g carbo., 31 g fat, 62 mg cholesterol, 3 g dietary fiber, 1,583 mg sodium.

Chicken and Lime
Soup with Tortillas

Easy Ways to Peel Hot or Sweet Peppers

Follow one of these methods to loosen the skins of peppers so you can easily peel them:

- Roasting: Quarter peppers lengthwise; remove stems and seeds. Cut small slits into ends of pieces so they'll lie flat. Place pepper pieces, cut sides down, on a foil-lined baking sheet. Bake in a 425° oven for 20 to 25 minutes or until skins are bubbly and brown. Immediately place peppers in a clean brown paper bag; close bag tightly. Cool for 15 minutes, then peel the pepper pieces with a sharp knife.
- Broiling: Preheat broiler. Prepare peppers as directed for roasting method. Broil 4 inches from the heat for 8 to 10 minutes or until skins are bubbly and brown, turning once. Immediately place pepper pieces in a clean brown paper bag; close bag tightly. Cool for 15 minutes, then peel the pepper pieces with a sharp knife.

Stuffed Turkey

Preparation Time: 25 minutes
Roasting Time: 3½ hours
Standing Time: 15 minutes

8   ounces ground pork
½   cup chopped onion
1   clove garlic, minced
2   medium tomatoes, chopped
1   small green-tipped banana, peeled and chopped
1   tart apple, peeled, cored, and chopped
¼   cup raisins
2   tablespoons slivered almonds, toasted
1   pickled jalapeño pepper, rinsed, seeded, and chopped, or 2 tablespoons canned
       chopped green chile peppers
½   teaspoon salt
¼   teaspoon pepper
1   8- to 10-pound turkey
¼   cup margarine or butter, melted
½   cup dry white wine, chicken broth, or water
¼   cup all-purpose flour

━━━━ For stuffing, in a large skillet cook pork, onion, and garlic until meat is brown and onion is tender; stir to break up pork. Drain off fat. Stir in tomatoes, banana, apple, raisins, almonds, and jalapeño pepper. Cook and stir 2 minutes. Remove from heat; stir in salt and pepper. Cool slightly.

━━━━ Rinse turkey; pat dry. Spoon some of the stuffing loosely into the neck cavity; pull neck skin to back of bird and fasten securely with a small skewer. Lightly spoon the remaining stuffing into the body cavity. If opening has a band of skin across the tail, tuck the drumsticks under the band; if there is no band, tie the drumsticks securely to tail. Twist the wing tips under back.

━━━━ In a shallow roasting pan place bird, breast side up, on a rack. Brush with the melted margarine. If desired, insert a meat thermometer in center of inside thigh muscle, not touching bone. Cover bird loosely with foil. Roast in a 325° oven for 3½ to 4¾ hours, basting occasionally with pan drippings, until the meat thermometer registers 180° to 185° or until drumsticks move easily in their sockets and juices run clear. When bird is two-thirds done, cut band of skin or string between drumsticks so thighs will cook evenly. Uncover turkey during last 45 minutes of roasting. Let turkey stand, covered, for 15 minutes before carving.

Meanwhile, for the gravy, spoon excess fat from pan drippings; add water to remaining drippings to make 2 cups liquid. Pour liquid into a saucepan. Stir wine, chicken broth, or more water into flour; stir into liquid in saucepan. Cook and stir until mixture is thickened and bubbly; cook and stir for 2 minutes more. Pass gravy with turkey and stuffing. Makes 8 to 12 servings.

*Per serving: 418 cal., 39 g pro., 14 g carbo., 21 g fat, 113 mg cholesterol,
2 g dietary fiber, 296 mg sodium.*

Chicken in Almond and Tomatillo Sauce
Preparation Time: 45 minutes

6   medium skinless, boneless chicken breast halves
    Nonstick spray coating
2   teaspoons olive oil
1   medium onion, chopped
1   clove garlic, minced
4   ounces fresh tomatillos (4 or 5 medium), husked
1   2-ounce package slivered almonds
½   cup chicken broth
¼   cup orange juice
¼   cup dry white wine
¼   teaspoon salt
⅛   teaspoon pepper

Rinse chicken; pat dry. Spray an unheated 12-inch skillet with nonstick coating. In the skillet cook chicken over medium heat for 10 to 12 minutes or until tender and no longer pink, turning once. Remove chicken; cover to keep warm. Add olive oil, onion, and garlic to skillet; cook about 5 minutes or until onion is tender.

Meanwhile, quarter tomatillos. In a blender container place tomatillos, almonds, and onion mixture; cover and blend until almonds are finely ground. Add tomatillo mixture, chicken broth, orange juice, wine, salt, and pepper to skillet. Boil gently, uncovered, about 7 minutes or until sauce is desired consistency. Spoon sauce onto plates. Cut chicken breasts into ½-inch-thick slices; arrange on sauce. Makes 6 servings.

*Per serving: 206 cal., 22 g pro., 6 g carbo., 10 g fat, 54 mg cholesterol,
1 g dietary fiber, 220 mg sodium.*

Chicken with Pepper-Pumpkin Seed Mole

Pumpkin seeds, sometimes called pepitas, are often sold in small bags. Look for them where dried Mexican peppers and spices are sold. They contribute a wonderful, nutty taste to the mole sauce. Complete your meal with slices of papaya and Mexican Rice (see recipe, page 70).

Standing Time: 45 minutes

Preparation Time: 20 minutes

2	dried ancho or pasilla peppers
1½	pounds skinless, boneless chicken breast halves (6) or turkey breast tenderloin steaks, cut into 6 portions
	Nonstick spray coating
¼	cup chicken broth
1	medium tomato, cut up
1	medium onion, cut up
⅓	cup pumpkin seeds or blanched almonds, toasted
2	cloves garlic
1	tablespoon sugar
2	teaspoons unsweetened cocoa powder
½	teaspoon ground coriander
¼	teaspoon salt
¼	teaspoon ground cinnamon
6	whole wheat flour tortillas, warmed (see tip, page 33)

▬ Rinse dried peppers in water. Slit peppers lengthwise; discard stems and seeds. With a knife or scissors, cut up peppers. In a bowl add pepper pieces to boiling water to cover; let stand for 45 to 60 minutes to soften. Drain well. Set aside.

▬ Rinse chicken or turkey; pat dry. Spray an unheated large skillet with nonstick coating. In the skillet cook chicken or turkey over medium heat for 10 minutes or until tender and no longer pink, turning once.

▬ For mole, in a blender container combine drained peppers, broth, tomato, onion, pumpkin seeds or almonds, garlic, sugar, cocoa powder, coriander, salt, and cinnamon. Cover and blend until nearly smooth, stopping blender to scrape sides as needed. Transfer to a small saucepan. Cook, uncovered, over medium-low heat about 5 minutes or until bubbly, stirring occasionally. Serve chicken with mole and warmed tortillas. Garnish with cilantro, pumpkin seeds, and chopped tomato, if desired. Serves 6.

Per serving: 273 cal., 31 g pro., 29 g carbo., 6 g fat, 72 mg cholesterol, 5 g dietary fiber, 399 mg sodium.

Chicken with Mushrooms

Cilantro, also called coriander or Chinese parsley, lends a distinctive flavor to the wine-based mushroom sauce.

Preparation Time: 30 minutes
Cooking Time: 35 minutes

2½ to 3 pounds meaty chicken pieces (breasts, thighs, and drumsticks)
1   tablespoon cooking oil
1   tablespoon margarine or butter
1   cup dry white wine or ½ cup chicken broth *and* ½ cup apple juice
3   cloves garlic, minced
2   tablespoons snipped fresh cilantro
½   teaspoon salt
¼   teaspoon pepper
8   ounces fresh mushrooms, sliced
4   green onions, chopped
     Fresh cilantro sprigs (optional)

━━━ Remove skin from chicken, if desired. Rinse the chicken; pat dry. In a 12-inch skillet cook chicken pieces in hot oil and margarine or butter over medium heat about 15 minutes, turning to brown evenly. Drain off fat.

━━━ In a mixing bowl stir together wine (or chicken broth and apple juice), garlic, and snipped cilantro. In the skillet sprinkle chicken with the salt and pepper. Add mushrooms, green onions, and wine mixture. Bring to boiling; reduce heat. Cover and simmer for 35 to 40 minutes or until chicken is tender and no longer pink. Transfer chicken and mushrooms to serving platter; cover to keep warm.

━━━ Bring mixture in skillet to boiling. Boil gently, uncovered, about 8 minutes or until reduced by about half (about 1¼ cups). Spoon mixture over chicken. Garnish with cilantro sprigs, if desired. Makes 6 servings.

Per serving: 348 cal., 32 g pro., 3 g carbo., 20 g fat, 100 mg cholesterol,
1 g dietary fiber, 291 mg sodium.

Chicken with Oranges

Serve this colorful entrée with hot cooked rice seasoned with snipped cilantro.

Preparation Time: 15 minutes

Cooking Time: 40 minutes

4	to 6 meaty chicken pieces (breasts, thighs, and drumsticks) (about 1½ pounds)
1	medium onion, cut up
1	tablespoon cooking oil
½	teaspoon salt
¼	teaspoon ground cinnamon
¼	teaspoon ground cloves
¼	teaspoon pepper
2	large cloves garlic, cut up
½	cup orange juice
2	tablespoons light raisins
1	tablespoon drained capers
	Dash ground saffron (optional)
1	orange, sliced
½	cup sliced almonds, toasted

—— Remove skin from chicken, if desired. Rinse chicken; pat dry. In a blender container combine the onion, cooking oil, salt, cinnamon, cloves, pepper, and garlic. Cover and blend until a paste forms. (If desired, finely chop the onion and garlic, and mix ingredients together by hand.) Rub onion paste over chicken parts.

—— Place the chicken in a 2-quart rectangular baking dish. Add the orange juice, raisins, capers, and, if desired, saffron. Cover and bake in a 350° oven for 20 minutes. Uncover and bake 20 to 25 minutes more or until chicken is tender and no longer pink. To serve, place chicken on serving platter and garnish with orange slices and almonds. Makes 4 servings.

Per serving: 393 cal., 31 g pro., 16 g carbo., 23 g fat, 88 mg cholesterol, 3 g dietary fiber, 387 mg sodium.

Arroz con Pollo

*A traditional favorite, this chicken dish with rice is an attractive main course that needs just a
fresh salad or relish and a beverage to complete the meal.*
Preparation Time: 35 minutes
Cooking Time: 30 minutes

1   2½- to 3-pound cut up broiler-fryer chicken
3   tablespoons olive oil
1¼ cups long grain rice
1   14½-ounce can chicken broth
1   12-ounce can beer
1   tablespoon ground cumin
2   cloves garlic, minced
½   teaspoon salt
¼   teaspoon ground saffron or ⅛ teaspoon ground turmeric
¼   teaspoon pepper
     Salt
     Pepper
2   10-ounce packages frozen peas

▬ Rinse chicken; pat dry. In a 12-inch skillet cook chicken, uncovered, in hot olive
oil over medium heat 15 minutes, turning to brown evenly. Remove chicken from skillet.

▬ To the skillet add *uncooked* rice. Cook and stir over medium heat until rice is
light brown. Carefully stir in broth, beer, cumin, garlic, the ½ teaspoon salt, saffron or
turmeric, and the ¼ teaspoon pepper.

▬ Place chicken on top of the rice mixture. Season lightly with additional salt and
pepper. Bring to boiling; reduce heat. Cover and simmer for 30 to 35 minutes or until rice
and chicken are tender and the chicken is no longer pink. Remove the chicken; keep
warm. Stir the peas into the rice mixture; heat through. Arrange the chicken on top of the
rice mixture; serve immediately. If desired, garnish with strips of red sweet pepper and
fresh basil. Makes 6 servings.

*Per serving: 493 cal., 29 g pro., 47 g carbo., 19 g fat, 67 mg cholesterol,
6 g dietary fiber, 651 mg sodium.*

Pasilla Chicken with Olives and Raisins

Although the peppers need to be soaked, you can brown the chicken while the peppers soften.
The olives are an interesting counterpart to the medium-hot fire in this dish.
Standing/Preparation Time: 45 minutes
Cooking Time: 55 minutes

2　dried pasilla peppers
1　3- to 3½-pound cut up broiler-fryer chicken
2　tablespoons olive oil or cooking oil
½　cup sliced onion
1　Anaheim pepper, seeded and chopped
⅓　cup water
1　7½-ounce can tomatoes, cut up
1　cup sliced carrots
⅓　cup raisins
¼　cup sliced pitted green olives

▬▬▬ Rinse dried peppers in water. In a bowl add peppers to boiling water to cover; let stand for 45 to 60 minutes to soften. Drain well. Cut in half and remove seeds. Scrape pulp from skin; set pulp aside. Discard skins.

▬▬▬ Remove skin from chicken. Rinse chicken; pat dry. In a large skillet cook chicken in hot oil over medium heat about 15 minutes, turning to brown evenly. Drain off fat. Add onion and Anaheim pepper; cook for 3 minutes. In a small bowl stir together the ⅓ cup water and pepper pulp; add to skillet along with *undrained* tomatoes, carrots, raisins, and olives. Bring to boiling; reduce heat. Cover and simmer for 30 minutes or until chicken is tender and no longer pink. Transfer chicken to serving platter; cover to keep warm.

▬▬▬ Boil cooking liquid gently about 3 minutes or until desired consistency. Skim fat from pan juices; spoon over chicken mixture on platter. Makes 6 servings.

Per serving: 399 cal., 35 g pro., 14 g carbo., 22 g fat, 108 mg cholesterol,
2 g dietary fiber, 315 mg sodium.

Creamy Seafood Enchiladas

Preparation Time: 25 minutes

Baking Time: 20 minutes

10 ounces shrimp in shells, peeled and deveined

1 8-ounce package cream cheese, softened

½ cup shredded Monterey Jack cheese (2 ounces)

2 tablespoons dry white wine

1 6-ounce can crabmeat, drained, flaked, and cartilage removed

1 4-ounce can diced green chile peppers, drained

¼ cup cooking oil

12 6-inch corn tortillas

½ cup sliced green onions

2 tablespoons margarine or butter

3 tablespoons all-purpose flour

¼ teaspoon salt

¼ teaspoon pepper

2 cups milk

1 cup shredded Monterey Jack cheese (4 ounces)

Sliced green onion

Paprika

▬ In a saucepan cook shrimp in boiling water about 3 minutes or until opaque. Drain; chop. For filling, combine cream cheese, the ½ cup Monterey Jack cheese, and wine. Beat with an electric mixer until almost smooth. Stir in crab, shrimp, and peppers.

▬ In a heavy skillet heat cooking oil. Dip tortillas, one at a time, in hot oil for 10 seconds or just until limp, adding more oil, if needed. Drain on paper towels. Spoon about ¼ *cup* filling onto each tortilla; roll up filled tortillas and place, seam side down, in a 3-quart rectangular baking dish.

▬ For sauce, in a medium saucepan cook the ½ cup green onions in margarine or butter until tender but not brown. Stir in flour, salt, and pepper. Add milk all at once. Cook and stir until mixture is thickened and bubbly. Pour sauce over tortillas.

▬ Bake, covered, in a 350° oven for 15 to 20 minutes or until heated through. Uncover; sprinkle with the 1 cup Monterey Jack cheese. Bake about 5 minutes more or until cheese melts. Garnish with green onion and paprika. Makes 6 servings.

Per serving: 610 cal., 29 g pro., 38 g carbo., 39 g fat, 166 mg cholesterol,
4 g dietary fiber, 889 mg sodium.

Chilled Fish in Escabeche Paste

Preparation Time: 15 minutes
Marinating Time: 1 hour

½ teaspoon dried oregano, crushed
¼ teaspoon ground cumin
¼ teaspoon ground cinnamon
⅛ teaspoon ground allspice
3 tablespoons olive oil or cooking oil
2 cloves garlic, minced
1 fresh jalapeño pepper, seeded and finely chopped
½ cup orange juice
½ cup chicken broth
3 tablespoons white vinegar
1 teaspoon sugar
1½ pounds fish fillets, such as red snapper, cod, sole, or orange roughy
1 cup sliced red onion
   Spinach or lettuce leaves
1 tomato, seeded and chopped

▬ In a small bowl stir together oregano, cumin, cinnamon, and allspice. In a large skillet heat *1 tablespoon* of the oil; add spice mixture, garlic, and jalapeño pepper. Cook and stir for 2 minutes. Stir in orange juice, broth, vinegar, and sugar. Bring to boiling; boil gently for 1 to 2 minutes. Remove escabeche mixture from heat and cool slightly.

▬ In another large skillet heat remaining 2 tablespoons oil. Cook fish in oil over medium-high heat about 5 minutes or until fish flakes when tested with a fork; turn once. Transfer fish to a shallow nonmetallic bowl.

▬ Arrange sliced onion over fish; spoon warm escabeche mixture over fish. Cover and marinate in the refrigerator for 1 to 2 hours, occasionally spooning sauce over fish. (Do not chill longer in marinade or fish will toughen.)

▬ To serve, arrange spinach leaves on a serving platter. Arrange fish pieces and onion over top. Spoon tomato over fish. Serve with marinade. Makes 4 to 6 servings.

Per serving: 301 cal., 35 g pro., 10 g carbo., 13 g fat, 60 mg cholesterol, 1 g dietary fiber, 231 mg sodium.

Chilled Fish in Escabeche Paste

20-Minute Chicken Tacos

Try using purchased taco shells for this fast-fixing treat, pictured on the cover.

Preparation Time: 20 minutes

8 taco shells or eight 6- to 8-inch flour or corn tortillas
12 ounces skinless, boneless chicken breasts
2 teaspoons chili powder
½ teaspoon garlic salt
½ teaspoon ground cumin
1 tablespoon cooking oil
1 medium tomato, chopped
1 cup finely shredded lettuce
1 cup shredded cheddar cheese (4 ounces)
   Bottled salsa and/or dairy sour cream

▬ To warm taco shells, place in a baking pan and heat in a 300° oven for 8 to 10 minutes before filling. (Or, to warm soft flour or corn tortillas, stack the tortillas and wrap tightly in foil. Heat in a 300° oven for 10 minutes to soften.)

▬ Meanwhile, rinse chicken; pat dry. Stir together the chili powder, garlic salt, and cumin. Rub mixture over both sides of chicken.

▬ In a large skillet cook chicken in hot oil over medium-high heat for 10 to 12 minutes or until chicken is tender and no longer pink, turning once. Shred chicken.

▬ To assemble tacos, place chicken in warm taco shells or place on soft flour or corn tortillas. Add tomato, lettuce, and cheese. Serve with salsa and/or sour cream. (If using soft flour or corn tortillas, roll them up.) Makes 4 servings.

Per serving: 381 cal., 27 g pro., 21 g carbo., 22 g fat, 74 mg cholesterol,
1 g dietary fiber, 697 mg sodium.

Snapper Veracruz

This flavorful entrée is generous on the sauce and goes well with accompaniments like potatoes,
noodles, or rice.
Preparation Time: 15 minutes
Cooking Time: 8 minutes

1	pound fresh or frozen red snapper fillets or other fish fillets
1	large onion, sliced and separated into rings
2	cloves garlic, minced
1	tablespoon cooking oil
1	16-ounce can tomatoes, cut up
¼	cup sliced pimiento-stuffed olives
¼	cup dry white wine
2	tablespoons capers, drained
1	tablespoon seeded and chopped canned jalapeño pepper or fresh jalapeño pepper, seeded and finely chopped
½	teaspoon sugar
1	bay leaf
	Several dashes ground cinnamon
¼	cup all-purpose flour
⅛	teaspoon salt
⅛	teaspoon pepper
1	tablespoon cooking oil

▬ Thaw fish, if frozen. For sauce, in a medium saucepan cook onion and garlic in 1 tablespoon hot cooking oil until onion is tender but not brown. Stir in *undrained* tomatoes, olives, wine, capers, jalapeño pepper, sugar, bay leaf, and cinnamon. Bring mixture to boiling. Boil gently, uncovered, for 5 to 7 minutes or until slightly thickened. Remove bay leaf.

▬ In a small mixing bowl stir together flour, salt, and pepper. Coat fillets on both sides with flour mixture. In a large skillet cook fish in 1 tablespoon hot oil over medium heat for 4 to 5 minutes on each side or until fish flakes easily when tested with a fork.

▬ To serve, arrange fish on a platter. Spoon sauce over top. Makes 4 servings.

Per serving: 253 cal., 25 g pro., 15 g carbo., 9 g fat, 40 mg cholesterol,
2 g dietary fiber, 498 mg sodium.

Garlic Shrimp

*This popular shrimp dish is commonly served in Mexico with crusty
bread or rice.*

Preparation Time: 10 minutes

2 tablespoons olive oil or cooking oil
1 pound large shrimp in shells, peeled and deveined
3 fresh or canned mild green chile peppers, rinsed, seeded, and finely chopped
3 to 4 cloves garlic, minced
½ teaspoon sugar
¼ teaspoon salt
   Fresh cilantro or parsley sprigs (optional)
   Mexican Rice (see recipe, page 70) (optional)

In a large skillet heat oil; cook shrimp, peppers, garlic, sugar, and salt in hot oil about 3 minutes or until shrimp turn opaque, stirring constantly. If desired, garnish with cilantro or parsley sprigs, and serve with Mexican Rice. Makes 4 servings.

*Per serving: 130 cal., 14 g pro., 2 g carbo., 7 g fat, 125 mg cholesterol,
0 g dietary fiber, 351 mg sodium.*

Tortilla Casserole

If desired, use a combination of Monterey Jack and cheddar cheeses.

Preparation Time: 15 minutes (plus salsa)

Baking Time: 25 minutes

6 6-inch corn tortillas
   Cooking oil for frying
2 cups shredded Monterey Jack cheese or cheddar cheese (8 ounces)
½ cup chopped onion
1½ cups Tomatillo Salsa (see recipe, page 17)
⅓ cup dairy sour cream

1   tablespoon water
1   medium avocado, halved, seeded, peeled, and thinly sliced
     Snipped fresh cilantro or parsley

■ Tear tortillas into 1½-inch pieces. In a heavy saucepan or deep skillet heat ½ inch of cooking oil. Fry tortilla pieces, *one-fourth to one-third at a time*, in hot oil for 45 to 60 seconds or until crisp and golden. Remove tortilla pieces with slotted spoon; drain on paper towels.

■ In a greased 2-quart square baking dish layer the tortillas, *half* of the cheese, the onion, and the Tomatillo Salsa. Sprinkle remaining cheese over top. Bake, covered, in a 350° oven about 25 minutes or until mixture is hot and bubbly.

■ In a small mixing bowl combine dairy sour cream and water; drizzle over top of the casserole. Garnish with avocado slices, and cilantro or parsley. Makes 4 servings.

Per serving: 552 cal., 19 g pro., 32 g carbo., 41 g fat, 59 mg cholesterol, 5 g dietary fiber, 601 mg sodium.

Bean Tostadas

Preparation Time: 5 minutes
Baking Time: 10 minutes

4   8-inch flour tortillas
2   cups refried beans
4   cups shredded lettuce
½   cup shredded reduced-fat Monterey Jack cheese (2 ounces)
½   cup light dairy sour cream
½   cup salsa

■ Place tortillas on a baking sheet. Bake in 375° oven for 10 to 15 minutes or until tortillas are dry and crisp, turning once.

■ Meanwhile, in a saucepan heat refried beans. Place tortillas on serving plates. Spread *one-fourth* of the beans over each tortilla. Top with *one-fourth* of the lettuce, cheese, sour cream, and salsa. Makes 4 servings.

Per serving: 349 cal., 18 g pro., 50 g carbo., 9 g fat, 18 mg cholesterol, 11 g dietary fiber, 998 mg sodium.

Huevos Rancheros

Toasted tortilla wedges are the perfect accompaniment for this Mexican classic. Arrange the tortilla wedges in a single layer on a baking sheet and bake in a 350° oven for 12 to 15 minutes or until crisp.

Preparation Time: 20 minutes
Cooking Time: 7 minutes

¼   cup finely chopped onion or green onions
2   cloves garlic, minced
2   tablespoons margarine or butter
1   15-ounce can tomato sauce
1   8-ounce can tomato sauce
¾   cup water
½   teaspoon crushed red pepper
½   teaspoon dried oregano, crushed
¼   teaspoon dried basil, crushed
8   eggs
    Corn tortillas, cut into wedges and toasted
1   large avocado, halved, seeded, peeled, and cubed

In a large skillet cook onion and garlic in margarine or butter until tender but not brown. Stir in tomato sauces, water, crushed pepper, oregano, and basil. Bring to boiling; reduce heat. Simmer for 4 minutes.

Carefully break *1 egg* into a small dish. Gently slide the egg into the sauce in the skillet. Repeat with remaining eggs, allowing each egg an equal amount of space.

Cover skillet and simmer gently for 7 to 8 minutes or until yolks are just set. Serve eggs and sauce with tortilla wedges and cubed avocado. Makes 4 servings.

Per serving: 411 cal., 18 g pro., 29 g carbo., 26 g fat, 426 mg cholesterol, 7 g dietary fiber, 1,176 mg sodium.

Casserole-Style Chiles Rellenos

Preparation Time: 25 minutes
Baking Time: 15 minutes
Standing Time: 5 minutes

2   fresh large poblano peppers or green sweet peppers (8 ounces)
1   cup shredded Monterey Jack cheese with jalapeño peppers (4 ounces)
3   beaten eggs
¼   cup milk
⅓   cup all-purpose flour
½   teaspoon baking powder
¼   teaspoon ground red pepper
⅛   teaspoon salt
¾   cup shredded cheddar cheese (3 ounces)
1   cup picante sauce
¼   cup dairy sour cream

▬ Quarter the peppers and remove stems, seeds, and veins. In a saucepan immerse peppers into boiling water for 3 minutes. Drain the peppers. Invert on paper towels to drain well. In a well-greased 1½-quart casserole place *half* of the peppers. Top with *half* of the shredded Monterey Jack cheese. Repeat layers.

▬ In a medium mixing bowl combine eggs and milk. Add flour, baking powder, ground red pepper, and salt. Beat until smooth. Pour egg mixture over peppers.

▬ Bake, uncovered, in a 450° oven for 15 minutes or until set. Sprinkle with the cheddar cheese. Let stand about 5 minutes or until cheese melts. Serve with picante sauce and dairy sour cream. Makes 4 servings.

Per serving: 353 cal., 20 g pro., 17 g carbo., 23 g fat, 215 mg cholesterol,
1 g dietary fiber, 848 mg sodium.

Cheese Enchiladas

Preparation Time: 30 minutes
Baking Time: 20 minutes
Standing Time: 10 minutes

¼ cup cooking oil
12 6-inch corn tortillas
2 cups shredded Monterey Jack cheese or cheddar cheese (8 ounces)
¾ cup finely chopped onion
3 tablespoons margarine or butter
¼ cup all-purpose flour
1 8-ounce carton dairy sour cream
2 cups chicken broth
1 4-ounce can diced green chile peppers, drained

▬ In a small skillet heat oil. Dip each tortilla in hot oil for 10 seconds or just until limp. Drain on paper towels. Place about *2 tablespoons* of the shredded cheese and *1 tablespoon* onion on each tortilla; roll up and place, seam side down, in a 2-quart rectangular baking dish.

▬ For sauce, in a medium saucepan melt margarine. Combine flour and sour cream; stir in broth. Add to melted margarine in saucepan. Cook and stir until thickened and bubbly; stir in drained peppers.

▬ Pour sauce over rolled tortillas in baking dish. Bake, covered, in a 425° oven for 15 minutes. Uncover; sprinkle with remaining cheese. Bake 5 minutes more. Let stand for 10 minutes before serving. Makes 6 servings.

Per serving: 528 cal., 16 g pro., 38 g carbo., 36 g fat, 50 mg cholesterol,
4 g dietary fiber, 909 mg sodium.

Lower-Fat Cheese Enchiladas: Prepare *Cheese Enchiladas* as directed above, *except* omit cooking tortillas in oil and rolling them. For sauce, reduce margarine to 2 tablespoons. Use reduced-fat cheese and light dairy sour cream. Alternately layer tortillas, 1½ cups of the cheese, and onions in baking dish, tearing tortillas to fit dish. Pour sauce on top. Bake, covered, for 20 minutes. Uncover; sprinkle with remaining cheese. Bake 5 minutes more. Let stand for 10 minutes before serving.

Per serving: 345 cal., 17 g pro., 38 g carbo., 16 g fat, 32 mg cholesterol,
4 g dietary fiber, 924 mg sodium.

SIDE
SENSATIONAL
DISHES

If you've ever been to Mexican markets, you know that they are brimming with fresh fruits and vegetables. So it's no wonder these foods are an essential part of a Mexican meal. Sometimes vegetables and salads are served as separate dishes in themselves; at other meals a combination of vegetables is sprinkled over the hot main dish. Salad ingredients or lightly cooked vegetables are often rolled into tortillas.

In this chapter, we present true-to-life Mexican side dishes that start with rice, beans, and corn, and other typical vegetables. Try Stuffed Chayotes (pictured). You'll also find a popular bread.

Stuffed Chayotes

You can prepare the stuffed chayotes several hours ahead. Just cover and refrigerate. To serve, heat the chilled chayotes in the oven, adding about 15 minutes to the baking time. (Pictured on pages 64–65.)

Preparation Time: 30 minutes
Baking Time: 5 minutes

2   medium chayotes or zucchini
1   tablespoon olive oil or cooking oil
⅓   cup chopped green onions
1   clove garlic, minced
1   large tomato, chopped
1   fresh Anaheim pepper, seeded and finely chopped, or ½ of a 4-ounce can diced
        green chile peppers, drained (about ¼ cup)
½   teaspoon dried oregano, crushed
⅛   teaspoon salt
⅛   teaspoon pepper
½   cup shredded cheddar cheese or Monterey Jack cheese (2 ounces)

━━━ Peel chayotes. Halve chayotes or zucchini lengthwise. Remove seeds from chayotes. Scoop out interior of chayotes or zucchini with a melon baller or grapefruit knife, leaving a ¼-inch-thick shell. Chop the chayote or zucchini pulp; set aside.

━━━ In a saucepan cook vegetable shells in lightly salted boiling water, 15 to 20 minutes for chayotes and about 3 minutes for zucchini or until tender, but not mushy. Drain; turn cut side down on paper towels.

━━━ Meanwhile, in a medium skillet heat olive oil. Cook green onions and garlic in hot oil for 3 minutes or until onion is tender but not brown. Add chayote or zucchini pulp, tomato, Anaheim pepper, oregano, salt, and pepper. Cook for 5 minutes more. Remove the skillet from the heat.

━━━ In a lightly greased 2-quart rectangular baking dish place chayote or zucchini shells, cut side up. Spoon vegetable filling mixture into each shell. Sprinkle with cheese. Bake, covered, in a 400° oven for 5 to 10 minutes or until filling is heated through and cheese is melted. Makes 4 servings.

Per serving: 119 cal., 5 g pro., 7 g carbo., 9 g fat, 15 mg cholesterol,
1 g dietary fiber, 160 mg sodium.

Stuffed Zucchini Squash

Preparation Time: 30 minutes
Cooking Time: 5 minutes

2   medium zucchini (about 12 ounces total)
1   tablespoon margarine, butter, or olive oil
1   small tomato, peeled and chopped
½   cup chopped fresh mushrooms
1   green onion, finely chopped
1   clove garlic, minced
2   tablespoons fine dry seasoned bread crumbs
2   tablespoons grated Mexican grating cheese or Parmesan cheese
    Grated Mexican grating cheese or Parmesan cheese

▬ In a large saucepan cook zucchini in boiling water for 10 minutes or until almost tender. Drain and cool slightly. Halve and carefully remove pulp, leaving a ¼-inch-thick shell. Chop pulp; set aside.

▬ In a medium skillet heat margarine. Cook tomato, mushrooms, green onion, and garlic in hot margarine until tender and most of the liquid has evaporated. Stir in zucchini pulp. Remove from heat.

▬ Stir in bread crumbs and the 2 tablespoons cheese. Spoon mixture into the zucchini shells. Sprinkle with additional grated cheese.

▬ Place on the unheated rack of a broiler pan. Broil about 4 inches from the heat for 5 minutes or until cheese is lightly browned. Makes 4 servings.

Per serving: 86 cal., 5 g pro., 7 g carbo., 5 g fat, 5 mg cholesterol,
2 g dietary fiber, 229 mg sodium.

Keeping Cool as Flavors Heat Up

If you're suffering from hot pepper fire-in-the-mouth, use milk or yogurt to quench the flames. Whole milk is better than skim, since the oils that give peppers their hot zing dissolve in fat. Soda pop or water will only act to spread the heat. Drinking beer or sucking on lemon or lime wedges also works to cool the heat. The hot pepper oils will dissolve in alcohol or citrus juices for quick relief.

Corn Pudding

This savory pudding is likely to be served as a separate course before the main dish. Try it in a Mexican menu, or serve it as a surprising accompaniment to grilled meat or poultry.

Preparation Time: 25 minutes

Baking Time: 30 minutes

1   **tablespoon cornmeal**
4   **fresh ears of corn**
1½ **cups milk**
3   **tablespoons margarine or butter, softened**
2   **teaspoons sugar**
3   **egg yolks**
½   **teaspoon baking powder**
¼   **teaspoon salt**
     Dash pepper
2   **egg whites**
     Red Chile Sauce (see recipe, page 16) or bottled salsa
     Cilantro (optional)

▬ Grease a 2-quart square baking dish; sprinkle cornmeal over bottom and sides of dish. Set aside.

▬ Husk corn and remove strings. Cut corn kernels from cobs (you should have 1¾ cups cut corn). In a blender container or food processor bowl blend or process the cut corn with ½ cup of the milk until mixture is nearly smooth.

▬ In a bowl beat together softened margarine and sugar on medium speed of an electric mixer until fluffy. Add egg yolks, one at a time, beating well after each addition. Fold in corn puree, the remaining 1 cup milk, the baking powder, salt, and pepper.

▬ Wash beaters. In another bowl beat egg whites on high speed until stiff peaks form (tips stand straight). Fold egg whites into corn mixture. Pour mixture into the prepared baking dish.

▬ Bake in a 350° oven about 30 minutes or until a knife inserted near the center comes out clean. Serve with Red Chile Sauce or salsa, about 2 tablespoons per serving. Garnish with cilantro, if desired. Makes 4 or 5 servings.

Per serving (with Red Chile Sauce): 302 cal., 10 g pro., 31 g carbo., 17 g fat, 167 mg cholesterol, 5 g dietary fiber, 461 mg sodium.

Corn Pudding

Corn in Mexican Cuisine

Grown by the ancients in Latin America, corn is the backbone of Mexican cuisine and appears in many different types of dishes.

The corn husks are used to wrap tamales. Fresh corn kernels are used in soups and vegetable dishes, such as the pudding recipe, at left, and the dried kernels are ground for masa, which goes into tortillas. Some Mexicans even steep the corn silks for a healing brewed tea.

Green Rice

Preparation Time: 20 minutes
Cooking Time: 15 minutes

½ cup fresh parsley leaves
½ cup fresh cilantro or parsley leaves
½ cup chopped onion
¼ cup water
1 fresh or canned mild green chile pepper, rinsed, seeded, and cut up
1 tablespoon lemon juice
2 cloves garlic, quartered
2 tablespoons olive oil or cooking oil
1 cup long grain rice
2 cups chicken broth

▬▬ In a blender container or food processor bowl combine parsley, cilantro or parsley, onion, water, pepper, lemon juice, and garlic. Cover and blend or process until mixture is nearly smooth, stopping and scraping sides as necessary.

▬▬ In a large skillet heat oil. Stir in *uncooked* rice; cook and stir about 5 minutes or until rice is golden brown. Heat chicken broth to boiling. Carefully add parsley mixture and boiling chicken broth to skillet. Cover and simmer for 15 to 20 minutes or until rice is tender and liquid is absorbed. Makes 4 servings.

*Per serving: 259 cal., 5 g pro., 41 g carbo., 8 g fat, 0 mg cholesterol,
1g dietary fiber, 513 mg sodium.*

Mexican Rice

Preparation Time: 20 minutes

1 large green sweet pepper, coarsely chopped
1 large tomato, coarsely chopped
1 medium onion, chopped
2 tablespoons margarine or butter
2 cups cooked rice

⅓   **cup water**
½   **teaspoon salt**
¼   **teaspoon pepper**

━━━   In a large saucepan cook green pepper, tomato, and onion in hot margarine or butter until vegetables are tender. Stir in cooked rice, water, salt, and pepper. Heat through, stirring occasionally. Makes 6 servings.

Per serving: 137 cal., 2 g pro., 23 g carbo., 4 g fat, 0 mg cholesterol,
1 g dietary fiber, 213 mg sodium.

Baked Hominy Casserole

Hominy is actually whole corn kernels that are dried with the hull and germ removed. It has a slightly sweet, cornlike flavor.

Preparation Time: 15 minutes
Baking Time: 35 minutes

1   **15-ounce can white or golden hominy, drained**
1   **cup shredded cheddar cheese (4 ounces)**
½   **cup dairy sour cream or light dairy sour cream**
1   **4-ounce can diced green chile peppers, drained**
½   **of a red sweet pepper, cut into ½-inch pieces**
4   **green onions, finely chopped**
2   **tablespoons milk**
1   **serrano pepper, chopped (optional)**
¼   **cup fine dry bread crumbs**
1   **tablespoon margarine or butter, melted**

━━━   In a large mixing bowl combine the hominy, cheese, sour cream, drained peppers, red sweet pepper, green onions, milk, and serrano pepper. Transfer mixture to a 1-quart casserole. Combine the bread crumbs and melted margarine or butter; sprinkle over top of hominy mixture.

━━━   Bake, uncovered, in a 350° oven for 35 to 40 minutes or until mixture is heated through. Makes 6 servings.

Per serving: 206 cal., 8 g pro., 15 g carbo., 13 g fat, 29 mg cholesterol,
1 g dietary fiber, 584 mg sodium.

Mexican Rolls

Introduced by the French, these oval-shaped rolls are commonly known as bolillos. In Mexico, they're typically served at breakfast or with the main meal entrée.

Preparation Time: 40 minutes
Rising Time: 1¾ hours
Baking Time: 25 minutes

3½ to 4 cups all-purpose flour
1   package active dry yeast
1   tablespoon sugar
½   teaspoon salt
1½ cups warm water (120° to 130°)
     Cornmeal
1   egg white
1   tablespoon milk or water

▬   In a large mixer bowl combine *1½ cups* of the flour, the yeast, sugar, and salt. Add warm water. Beat with an electric mixer on low to medium speed for 30 seconds, scraping sides of bowl. Beat on high speed for 3 minutes. Stir in as much of the remaining flour as you can with a wooden spoon.

▬   On a lightly floured surface, knead in enough of the remaining flour to make a stiff dough that is smooth and elastic (8 to 10 minutes). Shape dough into a ball. Place dough in a greased bowl; turn once to grease surface. Cover; let rise in a warm place until double (about 1 hour).

▬   Punch dough down. Turn out onto a lightly floured surface. Divide dough into 12 portions. Shape each into an oval about 5 inches long. Pull and twist ends slightly. Sprinkle cornmeal over 2 greased baking sheets. Transfer rolls to baking sheets. Use a sharp knife to make a ¼-inch-deep cut down the center of each roll.

▬   In a small bowl combine egg white and milk or water; brush over tops and sides of rolls. Cover and let rise till nearly double (about 45 minutes). Bake in a 375° oven for 15 minutes. Brush tops and sides again with egg-white mixture. Bake about 10 minutes more or until golden brown. Cool on wire racks. Makes 12 rolls.

Per roll: 144 cal., 4 g pro., 30 g carbo., 0 g fat, 0 mg cholesterol,
1 g dietary fiber, 95 mg sodium.

Mexican Boiled Beans

Serve these as a side dish, or use them for making Refried Beans, below. For a spicier version, substitute a jalapeño pepper for the Anaheim pepper.

Standing Time: 1 hour
Preparation Time: 15 minutes
Cooking Time: 1½ hours

2   cups dry pinto beans
1   medium onion, chopped
1   tomato, peeled and quartered
1   fresh Anaheim pepper, roasted (see tip, page 43), peeled,and chopped
2   cloves garlic, minced
1   teaspoon salt

▬ Rinse beans. In a Dutch oven combine beans and 6 cups *cold water*. Bring to boiling; reduce heat. Simmer for 2 minutes. Remove from heat. Cover and let stand for 1 hour. (Or, omit simmering; soak beans in cold water overnight in a covered container.) Drain and rinse.

▬ In the same pan combine drained beans, onion, tomato, pepper, garlic, salt, and 6 cups *fresh water*. Bring to boiling; reduce heat. Cover and simmer for 1½ hours or until beans are tender. Drain; if planning to make Refried Beans, reserve the cooking liquid. Makes 8 servings.

Per serving: 170 cal., 10 g pro., 32 g carbo., 1 g fat, 0 mg cholesterol, 14 g dietary fiber, 272 mg sodium.

Refried Beans

Dieters also can enjoy this flavorful accompaniment. To cut calories and fat, use just 1 tablespoon of bacon drippings, lard, or oil.

Preparation Time: 15 minutes

    Mexican Boiled Beans (see recipe, above)
3   tablespoons bacon drippings, lard, or cooking oil
    Shredded cheddar or Monterey Jack cheese

Drain cooked beans, reserving liquid. Heat bacon drippings, lard, or oil in a 12-inch skillet until hot. Carefully add beans. Using a potato masher, mash bean mixture completely. Add enough reserved liquid until desired consistency (about ¼ cup). Heat through. Serve with cheese and season to taste, if desired. Makes 6 to 8 servings.

Per serving (without cheese): 289 cal., 13 g pro., 43 g carbo., 8 g fat,
7 mg cholesterol, 18 g dietary fiber, 400 mg sodium.

Black Beans

Standing Time: 1 hour
Preparation Time: 20 minutes
Cooking Time: 1 hour

1   **cup dry black beans**
1   **dried chipotle or de árbol pepper (optional)**
2   **tablespoons cooking oil**
½   **cup chopped onion**
2   **to 4 cloves garlic, minced**
½   **teaspoon salt**
½   **teaspoon dried oregano, crushed**

Rinse beans. In a 3-quart saucepan combine beans and 6 cups *cold water.* Bring to boiling; reduce heat. Simmer for 2 minutes. Remove from heat. Cover and let stand for 1 hour. (Or, omit simmering; soak beans in cold water overnight in a covered container.) Drain and rinse.

If using pepper, cut open and discard stem and seeds; cut or crumble pepper into small pieces. In the same pan combine drained beans and 4 cups *fresh water.* In a small skillet heat cooking oil. Cook onion and garlic in hot oil for 5 minutes. Add vegetable mixture and pepper, if using, to bean mixture. Stir in salt and oregano.

Bring mixture to boiling; reduce heat. Cover and simmer for 1 to 1½ hours or until beans are tender, stirring occasionally. If desired, use a potato masher or back of a large spoon to mash beans slightly. Makes 4 servings.

Per serving: 226 cal., 11 g pro., 31 g carbo., 8 g fat, 0 mg cholesterol,
7 g dietary fiber, 269 mg sodium.

Rice with Vegetables and Pepper

Preparation Time: 15 minutes
Cooking Time: 15 minutes

2   tablespoons olive oil or cooking oil
½   cup chopped onion
1   Anaheim pepper, seeded and finely chopped
2   cloves garlic, minced
⅔   cup long grain rice
1⅓ cups chicken broth
1   cup shredded carrot
1   medium zucchini, cut into ½-inch cubes (1 cup)
½   cup fresh or frozen peas

━━━ In a large skillet heat oil. Cook onion, pepper, and garlic in hot oil about 3 minutes or until onion is tender. Stir in *uncooked* rice; cook and stir about 5 minutes or until rice just begins to brown. Drain off fat.

━━━ Carefully stir in broth, carrot, zucchini, and peas. Bring mixture to boiling; reduce heat. Cover and simmer about 15 minutes or until rice is tender and liquid is absorbed. Makes 4 servings.

Per serving: 235 cal., 5 g pro., 36 g carbo., 8 g fat, 0 mg cholesterol,
3 g dietary fiber, 375 mg sodium.

Rice with Vegetables and Pepper

Cabbage and Sweet Pepper Slaw

Purchase preshredded cabbage if you need to save on the prep time.

Preparation Time: 20 minutes

- 6 cups finely shredded cabbage
- 1 medium red sweet pepper, cut into thin strips (1 cup)
- 1 medium yellow sweet pepper, cut into thin strips (1 cup)
- 1 medium green sweet pepper, cut into thin strips (1 cup)
- 1 small red onion, thinly sliced
- ⅓ cup cider vinegar
- ⅓ cup salad oil
- 1 teaspoon sugar
- ½ teaspoon salt
- ¼ teaspoon ground cumin
- ⅛ teaspoon pepper

In a large bowl place cabbage, sweet peppers, and onion.

For dressing, combine vinegar, oil, sugar, salt, cumin, and pepper.

Pour dressing over the cabbage mixture and mix well. Slaw keeps overnight in a covered container in the refrigerator. Makes 8 to 10 servings.

Per serving: 110 cal., 1 g pro., 7 g carbo., 9 g fat, 0 mg cholesterol, 1 g dietary fiber, 144 mg sodium.

Salad with Jicama

Preparation Time: 25 minutes
Chilling Time: 1 hour

2   cups peeled jicama cut into bite-size sticks
2   oranges, peeled and sectioned
¼   cup sliced green onions
1   tablespoon finely shredded orange peel
⅓   cup orange juice
2   tablespoons lemon juice
1   tablespoon snipped fresh cilantro or parsley
     Dash salt
     Dash pepper
     Red leaf lettuce leaves or lettuce leaves

▬▬ In a medium bowl toss together jicama, oranges, and green onions. In a small bowl stir together orange peel, orange juice, lemon juice, cilantro or parsley, salt, and pepper. Add to jicama mixture and toss to coat.

▬▬ Cover and chill in the refrigerator at least 1 hour to blend flavors. To serve, line a serving bowl with lettuce leaves; spoon salad onto lettuce. Makes 4 or 5 servings.

Per serving: 72 cal., 2 g pro., 17 g carbo., 0 g fat, 0 mg cholesterol,
4 g dietary fiber, 38 mg sodium.

Vegetables Mexican-Style

To jazz up everyday entrées, take your cue from Mexican cooks, who use colorful shredded or finely chopped fresh vegetables, such as jicama, cucumbers, radishes, avocados, and lettuces, as accompaniments. Or, add fresh vegetables to salsas and use the salsas to spice up grilled meats, poultry, or fish.

Christmas Eve Salad

Don't wait for the holidays to serve this festive, brilliantly colored salad. It's great even if pomegranates are not in season. When they're not available, substitute chopped peanuts.

Preparation Time: 30 minutes

1   **8-ounce can pineapple chunks or ¼ fresh pineapple**
2   **large oranges**
1   **medium banana**
1   **large apple or ½ medium jicama**
1   **8-ounce can sliced beets, drained, or 2 medium beets,**
     cooked, peeled, and sliced
     Lettuce leaves
⅓   **cup pomegranate seeds or ½ cup coarsely chopped peanuts**
¼   **cup orange juice**
2   **tablespoons sugar**
     Dash salt

▬ Drain canned pineapple, or peel fresh pineapple quarter, remove eyes and core, and cut pineapple into chunks.

▬ Finely shred enough *orange peel* to make 1 teaspoon; set aside. Peel oranges; section over a bowl to catch juices. Peel and slice banana. Core and slice apple, or peel and thinly slice jicama. Toss apple (if used) and banana with orange sections and *orange juice* that was caught in bowl.

▬ Drain oranges, banana, and apple (if used); arrange with pineapple chunks, sliced beets, and jicama (if used) on a large lettuce-lined platter. Sprinkle with pomegranate seeds or peanuts.

▬ For dressing, combine the ¼ cup orange juice, sugar, reserved orange peel, and salt. Drizzle dressing over salad. Makes 4 or 5 servings.

*Per serving: 172 cal., 2 g pro., 43 g carbo., 1 g fat, 0 mg cholesterol,
5 g dietary fiber, 191 mg sodium.*

Tomatillo Salad
Preparation Time: 20 minutes

    Lettuce leaves
3 **medium tomatillos**
2 **medium tomatoes, sliced**
1 **medium red onion, cut into thin wedges**
2 **tablespoons snipped fresh cilantro or parsley**
2 **tablespoons vinegar**
2 **tablespoons olive oil or salad oil**
¼ **teaspoon pepper**
    Dash salt

 Line 4 individual salad plates with lettuce leaves. Remove husks from tomatillos; slice tomatillos crosswise. Arrange tomatillos, tomatoes, and onion on lettuce. For dressing, combine cilantro or parsley, vinegar, oil, pepper, and salt. Drizzle dressing over salads. Makes 4 servings.

*Per serving: 96 cal., 2 g pro., 7 g carbo., 7 g fat, 0 mg cholesterol,
1 g dietary fiber, 40 mg sodium.*

Shortcut Salad Ingredients

No time to wash and tear lettuce? Purchase a bagful of the mixed lettuce combos now found in supermarket produce sections. These colorful lettuce mixes are easy to toss in a salad bowl or use them to line a platter for a colorful arranged salad.

Other salad shortcuts available in the produce section include a coleslaw mix made with shredded cabbage and carrot and broccoli slaw, which is shredded broccoli mixed with shredded carrot.

Smiling Salad

Smiling Salad

Turn this into a main-dish salad by adding 3 cups of cubed, cooked chicken or fish.

Preparation Time: 35 minutes

    Torn mixed salad greens
2   **medium avocados, halved, seeded, peeled, and sliced**
2   **large grapefruit or 4 oranges, peeled and sectioned**
2   **small papayas, halved, seeded, peeled, and sliced**
    Poppy Seed Dressing (see recipe below)
    Jicama, cut into julienne strips (optional)
1   **large cluster black or Tokay grapes**

Line a platter or 6 individual plates with salad greens. Arrange avocado slices, grapefruit or orange sections, and papaya slices on greens. Spoon Poppy Seed Dressing over top. Sprinkle with jicama, if desired. Garnish with grapes. Makes 6 servings.

Poppy Seed Dressing: In a bowl or blender container combine ½ cup *salad oil,* ¼ cup *sugar,* 2 tablespoons *vinegar,* 2 tablespoons *honey mustard,* 2 tablespoons *lemon juice,* and 2 teaspoons *poppy seed.* Whisk together, or cover and blend until combined. Store, covered, in the refrigerator. Before serving, whisk until combined. Makes 1 cup.

Per serving: 401 cal., 3 g pro., 37 g carbo., 30 g fat, 0 mg cholesterol, 6 g dietary fiber, 73 mg sodium.

S W E E T S

IRRESISTIBLE

A menu from a Mexican restaurant, with its brief listing of desserts (typically flan, ice cream, or fresh fruit), belies the amazing variety of sweets *(dulces)* served on streets and in homes of Mexico. The candies and desserts (and sweet beverages, too) seem as varied as the rest of the native cuisine, and frequently they are tied into holiday traditions.

Our Mexican *dulces* are as simple to make as they are authentic. Sample Fried Plantains in Caramel Rum Sauce, Mexican Sugar Cookies, and Mexican Bread Pudding (a dish served during Lent). Almond Cake is often served at weddings in the Yucatan region. Or, try Buñuelos, rolled-out fritters served in a cinnamon syrup, and Flan (pictured), the all-time favorite.

Flan

Caramelized sugar pools around a delicate baked custard for this traditional dessert. (Pictured on pages 82–83.)

Preparation Time: 20 minutes
Baking Time: 35 minutes
Cooling Time: 1 hour
Chilling Time: 2 hours

⅓ **cup sugar**
4 **eggs**
½ **cup sugar**
2 **cups milk**
1½ **inches stick cinnamon**
¾ **teaspoon vanilla**
3 **whole strawberries, sliced (optional)**
   Mint leaves (optional)

�▬ To caramelize sugar, in a small heavy skillet heat the ⅓ cup sugar over medium heat until the sugar begins to melt *(do not stir until sugar begins melting)*. Cook and stir for 4 to 5 minutes more or until the sugar turns a rich brown. Remove skillet from heat and immediately pour caramelized sugar into an 8x1½-inch round baking pan. Holding pan with pot holders, quickly rotate pan so sugar coats the bottom and sides evenly. Cool.

▬ In a large mixing bowl beat eggs with a rotary beater, gradually adding the ½ cup sugar. In a saucepan heat milk and stick cinnamon over medium heat until mixture bubbles. Remove cinnamon. Slowly add milk to egg mixture, stirring constantly. Stir in vanilla.

▬ Place caramel-coated pan in a 13x9x2-inch baking pan on an oven rack. Pour egg mixture into round pan. Pour the hottest tap water available into the 13x9x2-inch baking pan around the round pan to a depth of about ½ inch.

▬ Bake, uncovered, in a 325° oven about 35 minutes or until a knife inserted halfway between the center and edge comes out clean. Carefully remove pan from hot water. Cool on a wire rack. Cover and chill in the refrigerator.

▬ To unmold flan, loosen edges with a spatula and slip end of spatula down sides of pan to let in air. Invert flan onto a serving platter. Spoon caramel mixture that remains in pan on top. Garnish with strawberries and mint leaves, if desired. Makes 6 servings.

Per serving: 198 cal., 7 g pro., 32 g carbo, 5 g fat, 148 mg cholesterol, 0 g dietary fiber, 83 mg sodium.

Fried Plantains in Caramel Rum Sauce

Look for ripe plantains that have a black skin and are soft to the touch.

Preparation Time: 20 minutes

Cooking Time: 5 minutes

4   **plantains or 6 firm bananas**

5   **tablespoons margarine or butter**

⅔   **cup packed brown sugar**

¼   **teaspoon ground nutmeg**

¼   **teaspoon rum extract or 3 tablespoons rum or orange liqueur**

     Sweetened Sour Cream or Crème Fraîche (see recipes below) or vanilla ice cream

■ Peel and cut plantains or bananas into ½-inch-thick slices. In a large skillet heat margarine or butter. Heat plantains or bananas in the margarine about 5 minutes for plantains or 2 minutes for bananas or just until warm.

■ Sprinkle with brown sugar. Stir gently until the sugar has melted. Add nutmeg and rum extract. (Or, if using rum or orange liqueur, heat in a small saucepan and pour liquor over plantain mixture, then carefully ignite.) Serve fruit with Sweetened Sour Cream, Crème Fraîche, or ice cream. Makes 6 servings.

Sweetened Sour Cream: In a small bowl stir together ¾ cup *dairy sour cream* and 1 tablespoon *sugar*. Makes ¾ cup.

Crème Fraîche: In a small saucepan heat 1 cup *whipping cream* (not ultra-pasteurized) over low heat until warm (90° to 100°). Pour the cream into a small bowl. Stir in 2 tablespoons *buttermilk*. Cover and let the mixture stand at room temperature for 24 to 30 hours or until the mixture is thickened. *Do not stir.* Store in a covered container in the refrigerator for up to a week. Stir before serving. Makes 1 cup.

Per serving (with Sweetened Sour Cream): 306 cal., 2 g pro., 43 g carbo, 16 g fat, 13 mg cholesterol, 2 g dietary fiber, 106 mg sodium.

Mexican Sugar Cookies

You can make these in traditional Mexican shapes as shown, or use your own cookie cutters to stamp out the dough.

Preparation Time: 30 minutes
Chilling Time: 1 hour
Baking Time: 14 minutes

1	cup lard, shortening, or butter
1	cup sugar
1	egg
¼	cup milk
3	cups all-purpose flour
2	teaspoons baking powder
1	teaspoon anise seed, crushed
¼	teaspoon salt
3	tablespoons brandy or orange juice
	Yellow food coloring
⅓	cup sugar
½	teaspoon ground cinnamon

▬▬▬ In a large mixing bowl beat lard on high speed of electric mixer for 30 seconds. Beat in the 1 cup sugar gradually until mixture is fluffy. Beat in egg and *2 tablespoons* of the milk until well mixed.

▬▬▬ In another bowl stir together flour, baking powder, anise seed, and salt. Gradually beat flour mixture into creamed mixture alternately with brandy or orange juice, beating well after each addition. (Dough should be smooth, pliable, and slightly stiff.) Tint *one-third* of the dough with yellow food coloring. Cover doughs; chill 1 to 2 hours or until easy to handle.

▬▬▬ On a lightly floured surface roll out dough as directed below. Cut into Turnovers or Sunbursts as directed below. Place cookies 1 inch apart on ungreased cookie sheets. Brush cookies with remaining 2 tablespoons milk. Combine ⅓ cup sugar and cinnamon; sprinkle over cookies. Bake in a 350° oven for 14 to 16 minutes or until edges of cookies are light golden brown. Cool on racks. Makes about 16.

▬▬▬ **Turnovers:** On a floured surface roll out white dough to ¼-inch thickness. With a large round cutter, cut dough into 3½-inch circles. Place a flattened 1-inch ball of yellow dough in the center of each circle. Fold each circle in half; seal edges with tines of a fork.

___ **Sunbursts:** On a floured surface roll out white dough to ½-inch thickness. Cut dough into rings with a 2½-inch doughnut cutter. Reroll scraps as necessary. Place rings on a cookie sheet. Using the yellow dough, make ½- to ¾-inch balls of dough. Place yellow balls in center of rings; flatten balls slightly to fill centers. Using the tines of a fork, decoratively score the edges of the cookies.

*Per cookie: 279 cal., 3 g pro., 35 g carbo, 14 g fat, 26 mg cholesterol,
1 g dietary fiber, 80 mg sodium.*

Mexican Hot Chocolate

For an even more authentic drink, purchase bars of Mexican chocolate, available in Mexican or Oriental markets. Then omit the cinnamon and almond extract, because the flavors already have been added to Mexican chocolate.

Preparation Time: 20 minutes

3   **ounces semisweet chocolate**
6   **cups milk**
3   **to 4 tablespoons brown sugar or granulated sugar**
1   **teaspoon ground cinnamon**
1   **teaspoon vanilla**
¼   **teaspoon almond extract**
    Whipping cream, whipped (optional)
    Ground cinnamon (optional)

___ Cut chocolate into pieces. In a large saucepan combine chocolate, *2 cups* of the milk, the sugar, and the 1 teaspoon cinnamon. Cook and stir over low heat until chocolate is melted. Stir in remaining milk, vanilla, and almond extract. Bring mixture just to a simmer, stirring constantly. Remove from heat and beat with a hand beater until frothy. (In Mexico a *molinillo*, a carved wooden tool, is used to whip a frothy top on the hot chocolate.) Pour hot chocolate into mugs and dollop with whipped cream, if desired. Sprinkle lightly with additional ground cinnamon, if desired. Makes 8 to 10 servings.

*Per serving: 155 cal., 7 g pro., 19 g carbo, 7 g fat, 14 mg cholesterol,
1 g dietary fiber, 93 mg sodium.*

Coffee with Milk
Preparation Time: 20 minutes

2½ cups water
½ cup ground coffee
3 inches stick cinnamon
6 whole cloves
2½ cups milk
2 to 4 tablespoons dark brown sugar

▬ Prepare strong coffee using the water, coffee, cinnamon, and cloves, following either the drip or percolator methods below.

▬ **For drip coffee,** line coffee basket with a filter. Measure coffee into lined basket and add the spices. For electric drip coffee maker, pour the cold water into upper compartment. Place pot on heating element and let water drip through basket. For nonelectric drip coffee maker, pour boiling water over coffee and spices in basket. Let water drip into pot.

▬ **For percolator coffee,** pour water into percolator. Stand stem and basket firmly in pot. Measure coffee and spices into basket. Replace basket lid and cover the pot. Bring water to boiling. Perk gently for 5 to 8 minutes. Remove basket and discard coffee grounds and spices.

▬ Meanwhile, in a medium saucepan heat milk. Stir sugar into coffee until sugar is dissolved. Stir coffee into hot milk and serve while hot. Makes 4 servings.

*Per serving: 96 cal., 5 g pro., 13 g carbo, 3 g fat, 11 mg cholesterol,
0 g dietary fiber, 81 mg sodium.*

Fruits of Mexico

Many of the most popular desserts in Mexican cuisine are laden with fruits (see pages 6–8). Here are two unusual types:

- **Cactus Pears**—Small, oval-shaped fruits from the nopal cactus, cactus pears are available in orange, pink, and yellow varieties, with a juicy texture and watermelonlike flavor. They also are called prickly pears.
- **Guavas**—Small, egg-shaped fruit with waxy, pale green to grey to yellow skins, depending on the variety. Fruit inside may be bright pink, white, or yellow, with sweet, heady flavor. Can be eaten seeds and all.

Mexican Bread Pudding

*This bread pudding is one of the most popular among a wide array of puddings and custards
served all over Mexico.*

Preparation Time: 25 minutes

Baking Time: 40 minutes

½ cup packed brown sugar

½ cup water

3 inches stick cinnamon

2 whole cloves

1 tablespoon margarine or butter

4 slices day-old bread, toasted and cubed

1 firm banana, sliced

2 apples, peeled, cored, and sliced

½ cup raisins

¼ cup peanuts, coarsely chopped

¼ cup blanched almonds, coarsely chopped

½ cup shredded Monterey Jack cheese (2 ounces)

  Crème Fraîche (see recipe, page 85) (optional)

_____ In a medium saucepan combine brown sugar, water, cinnamon, and cloves. Bring to
boiling; reduce heat. Boil gently about 8 to 10 minutes.

_____ Meanwhile, use the margarine or butter to grease a 2-quart square baking dish.
Using *half* of the ingredients, place a layer of bread, bananas, apples, raisins, peanuts, and
almonds. Repeat layers.

_____ Remove and discard spices from sugar syrup. *Gradually* pour syrup over bread and
fruit mixture, letting the bread absorb the syrup. (Pour slowly or the syrup will go to the bottom.)
Cover and bake in a 350° oven for 35 to 40 minutes or until apples are tender. Top with
cheese; bake 5 minutes longer. Serve with Crème Fraîche, if desired. Makes 6 to 8 servings.

*Per serving: 295 cal., 7 g pro., 44 g carbo, 11 g fat, 9 mg cholesterol,
3 g dietary fiber, 195 mg sodium.*

Almond Pudding with Custard Sauce

Preparation Time: 1 hour
Chilling Time: 4 hours

Nonstick spray coating
½ **cup sugar**
½ **envelope unflavored gelatin**
⅔ **cup water**
3 **egg whites**
⅛ **teaspoon almond extract**
Red food coloring
Green food coloring
3 **tablespoons finely chopped, blanched almonds**
3 **slightly beaten egg yolks**
2 **tablespoons sugar**
Dash salt
¾ **cup milk**
½ **teaspoon vanilla**

——— Spray a 9x5x3-inch loaf pan with nonstick coating; set aside. In the top of a double boiler combine the ½ cup sugar and gelatin; add water and egg whites. Cook and stir over hot water about 5 minutes or until the gelatin dissolves. Chill until partially set (consistency of unbeaten egg whites).

——— Add almond extract; beat at high speed of electric mixer for 3 to 4 minutes or until very light and tripled in volume. Remove *1½ cups* of the mixture; tint pink with 1 or 2 drops red food coloring. Spoon into bottom of prepared pan, spreading evenly. Chill 10 minutes. Divide remaining mixture in half. Tint *one half* green with 2 drops green food coloring; stir chopped almonds into remaining plain mixture. Spoon plain almond mixture over pink layer in pan. Chill 10 minutes. Add green layer. Cover; refrigerate several hours or overnight.

——— Meanwhile, for custard sauce, in a small saucepan combine egg yolks, the 2 tablespoons sugar, and salt. Add milk. Cook and stir over medium-low heat about 5 minutes or until sauce coats a metal spoon. Remove sauce from heat; stir in vanilla. Cover surface of custard with plastic wrap; chill.

——— To serve, unmold pudding onto a serving platter; cut into slices. Serve slices topped with custard sauce. Sprinkle toasted slivered almonds over top, if desired. Makes 8 servings.

Per serving: 122 cal., 4 g pro., 18 g carbo, 4 g fat, 82 mg cholesterol,
0 g dietary fiber, 50 mg sodium.

Rice Pudding

Preparation Time: 5 minutes
Cooking Time: 20 minutes

3   cups milk
½   cup long grain rice
3   inches stick cinnamon
½   cup raisins
¼   to ½ cup granulated sugar or packed brown sugar
1   teaspoon vanilla

In a heavy medium saucepan combine milk, *uncooked* rice, and cinnamon stick. Heat just to boiling; reduce heat. Cover and simmer about 20 minutes or until rice is tender. Remove cinnamon. Stir in raisins, sugar, and vanilla. Serve warm or cold. Makes 4 servings.

Per serving: 286 cal., 8 g pro., 56 g carbo, 4 g fat, 14 mg cholesterol, 1 g dietary fiber, 95 mg sodium.

Mango Chantilly Mousse

If mangoes are not available, you can substitute 1 cup puree made from papaya or nectarines, or a combination of the two.
Preparation Time: 25 minutes
Freezing Time: 1 hour
Standing Time: 15 minutes

2   ripe mangoes
1   orange
1   cup whipping cream
⅓   cup sifted powdered sugar
½   cup chopped toasted pecans

Cut flesh away from mango seeds by making a cut through each mango and sliding a sharp knife next to the seed along one side. Repeat on other side of the seed, resulting in two large pieces. Then cut away all of the meat remaining around the seed. Remove the peel.

Finely shred 2 teaspoons *orange peel*. Set orange peel aside. Peel and section the orange, discarding seeds. Crush the mangoes and oranges with a potato masher or process in a food processor or blender.

▬ In a medium mixing bowl combine the mashed fruit and shredded orange peel. In another bowl beat whipping cream until soft peaks form; beat in the powdered sugar. Gently fold whipped-cream mixture into mashed-fruit mixture. Spoon into dessert dishes. Cover and freeze for 1 to 2 hours or until ready to serve. To serve, remove from freezer and garnish with pecans. Let stand at room temperature about 15 minutes to soften slightly. Makes 6 servings.

Per serving: 252 cal., 2 g pro., 16 g carbo, 22 g fat, 54 mg cholesterol,
2 g dietary fiber, 16 mg sodium.

Mexican Chocolate Mousse

Preparation Time: 25 minutes
Cooling Time: 30 minutes
Chilling or Freezing Time: 4 hours

7   to 8 ounces Mexican-style sweet chocolate, cut up
2   cups whipping cream
1   tablespoon rum or ¼ teaspoon rum flavoring
1   teaspoon vanilla
¼   cup slivered or sliced almonds, toasted
     Fresh mint sprigs (optional)

▬ In a small heavy saucepan combine chocolate with ½ *cup* of the whipping cream. Stir over low heat until completely melted and the sugar in the chocolate is dissolved. [Or, to melt chocolate in a microwave oven, in a 2-cup microwave-safe measure or container place chocolate and ½ *cup* of the whipping cream. Micro-cook on 100% power (high) for 2 to 3 minutes or until chocolate is completely melted, stirring every 30 seconds.] Remove chocolate mixture from heat and cool. Add rum or rum flavoring and vanilla.

▬ Meanwhile, whip the remaining cream until soft peaks form. Fold melted chocolate into whipped cream. Spoon into dessert dishes. Cover and chill or freeze at least 4 hours or until ready to serve. To serve, garnish with almonds and fresh mint, if desired. Serves 8.

Per serving: 357 cal., 3 g pro., 17 g carbo, 33 g fat, 82 mg cholesterol,
1 g dietary fiber, 23 mg sodium.

Almond Cake

Preparation Time: 15 minutes
Baking Time: 30 minutes

2   eggs
1   cup sugar
½   cup milk
⅓   cup cooking oil
¾   cup all-purpose flour
¼   cup ground almonds
¾   teaspoon baking powder
¼   teaspoon salt
3   tablespoons sliced almonds, toasted
2   tablespoons almond liqueur (optional)
2   teaspoons sugar

▬ Grease and flour a 9-inch pie plate; set aside. In a large mixing bowl beat eggs with a fork until combined. Stir in the 1 cup sugar, milk, cooking oil, flour, ground almonds, baking powder, and salt; mix until combined.

▬ Pour batter into the prepared pie plate. Sprinkle sliced almonds on top. Bake in a 350° oven about 25 minutes or until a toothpick inserted near the center comes out clean.

▬ Remove cake from oven. If desired, brush almond liqueur over top of cake. Sprinkle with the 2 teaspoons sugar. Return to oven and bake for 5 minutes more. Remove to a wire rack. Cut into wedges; serve warm or cool. Makes 8 servings.

Per serving: 286 cal., 5 g pro., 37 g carbo, 14 g fat, 54 mg cholesterol,
1 g dietary fiber, 121 mg sodium.

Mexican Liqueurs

Mexican cooks often use liqueurs in making desserts and drinks. Almond, orange, and anise liqueurs are popular; so, too, is the well-known coffee liqueur. Some rums, brandies, and tequilas also are used.

Often the traditional almond cake is soaked with almond liqueur. Mixed candied and dried fruits might be steeped in rum or brandy before adding them to a baked dessert. Or mangoes, papayas, or pineapple may be flambéed with orange liqueur.

Buñuelos

Preparation Time: 30 minutes
Cooking Time (sauce): 30 minutes
Cooking Time (fritters): 18 minutes

1 **cup packed dark brown sugar**
3 **inches stick cinnamon**
1 **cup all-purpose flour**
⅛ **teaspoon baking powder**
　 Dash salt
2 **tablespoons shortening or lard**
　 Cooking oil for frying

▬ For syrup, in a small saucepan combine brown sugar and 1 cup *water*. Add cinnamon. Bring to boiling; reduce heat. Cook, uncovered, about 35 minutes or until thickened.

▬ Meanwhile, in a medium mixing bowl combine flour, baking powder, and salt. Cut in shortening until flour has a "cornmeal" feel. Make a well in center of dry ingredients; pour in ⅓ cup *warm water*. Mix well until a dough is formed. Knead about 5 minutes or until soft and smooth. Let dough rest 15 minutes. Shape into 12 balls. Pat balls flat; let rest while heating oil.

▬ In a deep saucepan heat oil to 365°. On lightly floured surface roll each ball to a 4-inch circle. Fry, one at a time, in hot oil about 45 seconds per side or until golden brown. Keep warm in a 300° oven while frying remaining. Serve with the syrup. Makes 12 servings.

Per serving: 168 cal., 1 g pro., 32 g carbo, 5 g fat, 0 mg cholesterol,
0 g dietary fiber, 24 mg sodium.

Ambrosia

Preparation Time: 10 minutes

▬ Chill 4 to 6 large *oranges*. Remove peel and white portion from oranges. Cut oranges crosswise into ¼-inch-thick slices, or thinner, if desired. Arrange orange slices on 4 or 6 dessert plates or in bowls. Sprinkle with ¼ teaspoon *ground cinnamon* and ¼ cup *shredded coconut*. If desired, garnish with fresh *mint sprigs*. Makes 4 to 6 servings.

Per serving: 94 cal., 2 g pro., 19 g carbo, 2 g fat, 0 mg cholesterol,
4 g dietary fiber, 17 mg sodium.

RECIPE INDEX

A-B

Almond Cake 94
Almond Pudding with
   Custard Sauce 91
Ambrosia 95
Avocado Soup, Chilled....................24
Baked Hominy Casserole 71
Bean Tostadas 59
Black Beans 75
Bread Pudding, Mexican 89
Buñuelos 95

C-E

Cabbage and Sweet Pepper Slaw 77
Casserole-Style Chiles Rellenos 62
Chayotes, Pork-Stuffed 36
Chayotes, Stuffed 66
Cheese Enchiladas 63
Chicken and Lime Soup with
   Tortillas 42
Chicken Dry Soup 41
Chicken in Almond and
   Tomatillo Sauce 45
Chicken Tacos, 20-Minute.................56
Chicken with Mushrooms 48
Chicken with Oranges 49
Chicken with Pepper-Pumpkin
   Seed Mole 47
Chile con Queso 29
Chiles Rellenos, Casserole-Style..........62
Chilled Avocado Soup 24
Chilled Fish in Escabeche Paste 54
Chocolate, Mexican Hot 87
Christmas Eve Salad.......................79
Chunky Guacamole 18
Coffee with Milk............................88
Cookies, Mexican Sugar...................86
Corn Pudding 68
Creamy Seafood Enchiladas 53
Crème Fraîche 85

F-M

Flan 84
Flank Steak, Peppered 33

Flank Steak Roll, Stuffed 32
Fried Cheese 28
Fried Plantains in Caramel
   Rum Sauce..............................85
Garlic Shrimp 58
Garlic Soup 22
Green Rice 70
Guacamole, Chunky........................18
Homemade Salsa 16
Hominy Casserole, Baked 71
Huevos Rancheros 61
Jicama with Chili and Lime 14
Josefinas 28
Lower-Fat Cheese Enchiladas 63
Mango Chantilly Mousse 92
Meatball Soup 37
Melon Punch 14
Mexican Boiled Beans 74
Mexican Bread Pudding 89
Mexican Chocolate Mousse 93
Mexican Hot Chocolate 87
Mexican Rice................................70
Mexican Rolls 73
Mexican-Style Shredded Pork 35
Mexican Sugar Cookies 86

N-R

Nachos with Chorizo 15
Pasilla Chicken with Olives
   and Raisins 52
Pepper-and-Cheese Quesadillas 21
Peppered Flank Steak......................33
Plantains in Caramel Rum
   Sauce, Fried.............................85
Poppy Seed Dressing 81
Pork Stew 40
Pork-Stuffed Chayotes 36
Pork Tostadas...............................35
Pumpkin and Tomato Soup 24
Quesadillas, Pepper-and-Cheese........21
Red Chile Sauce 16
Refried Beans................................74
Rice Pudding 92
Rolls, Mexican 73

S-Z

Salads

Cabbage and Sweet
   Pepper Slaw 77
Christmas Eve Salad.......................79
Salad with Jicama 78
Smiling Salad 81
Tomatillo Salad 80

Sausage-Stuffed Mushrooms 18
Seafood-Stuffed Chiles 27
Seviche-Style Crab and Scallops 26
Smiling Salad 81
Snapper Veracruz 57
Toasted Chili Nuts 19
Tomatillo Salsa 17
Tortilla Casserole 58
Turkey, Stuffed 44

Vegetables

Baked Hominy Casserole 71
Black Beans 75
Corn Pudding 68
Mexican Boiled Beans 74
Refried Beans 74
Rice with Vegetables and Pepper....76
Stuffed Chayotes 66
Stuffed Zucchini Squash 67

Vermicelli Soup 23
Zucchini Squash, Stuffed.................67

NUTRITIONAL FACTS

Each recipe in this book lists the nutritional values for one serving. Here's how we made our analyses.

When a recipe gives a choice of ingredients (such as margarine or butter) we used the first choice in our analysis.

Ingredients listed as optional were omitted from our calculations.

Finally, we rounded all values to the nearest whole number.